WITHDRAWN FROM
THE LIBRARY

UNIVERSITY OF
WINCHESTER

STRAIGHT UP

Straight Up concerns a young parolee sent by the local priest for rehabilitation to an apparently normal suburban family in South London. Given the willingness of father, mother and teenage daughter all to lead double lives of one kind or another, the explosive effect of his arrival is doubtless inevitable.

First presented at the Traverse Theatre, Edinburgh during the 1970 Edinburgh Festival, *Straight Up* marks the arrival in the British theatre of a talented new playwright. The *New York Times* called it 'a domestic comedy of horrifying undomesticity . . .' and *The Guardian* pronounced it 'a play with more truly funny lines and situations per minute than anyone has a right to expect'.

The photograph shows a scene Traverse *production and is reproduced by courtesy of Diane Tommes; the photograph on the back of the cover is reproduced by courtesy of Donald Cooper.*

KA 0039727 X

WITHDRAWN FROM
THE LIBRARY

UNIVERSITY OF
WINCHESTER

SYD CHEATLE

STRAIGHT UP

METHUEN & CO LTD
11 NEW FETTER LANE LONDON EC4

First published in 1971 by Methuen and Co Ltd
Copyright © 1971 by Syd Cheatle
Printed in Great Britain
by Cox & Wyman Ltd, Fakenham, Norfolk.

SBN 416 63290 4 Hardback
SBN 416 63300 5 Paperback

All rights whatsoever in this play are strictly reserved and application for performance, etc., should be made before rehearsal to Jonathan Clowes Ltd, 20 New Cavendish Street, London, W.1. No performance may be given unless a licence has been obtained.

This book is available in hardbound and paperback editions. The paperback edition is sold subject to the condition that it shall not, by way of trade or otherwise, be lent, resold, hired out, or otherwise circulated without the publisher's prior consent in any form of binding or cover other than that in which it is published and without similar condition including this condition being imposed on the subsequent purchaser.

KING ALFRED'S COLLEGE
CHESTER.

822.91
CHE

64063

Straight Up was first presented at the Traverse Theatre, Edinburgh on August 20 1970 with the following cast:

BERYL SEDLEY	Antonia Pemberton
FATHER HOOLIGAN	Peter Halliday
NED	Doug Fisher
SANDRA SEDLEY	Polly James
MICK	Tim Wylton
GEORGE SEDLEY	William Franklyn

Directed by Michael Rudman

The action takes place in the living-room of the Sedley home in S.E. London.

ACT ONE

The Sedley Living-room.
Early evening.
BERYL *ushers in* FATHER HOOLIGAN *from the hall.*

BERYL. It's in such a state. My husband uses it as a workroom
really.

HOOLIGAN. Not at all. Sure that's a powerful view you have there.
Isn't that the convent at the end of it?

BERYL. It backs right on to our garden.

HOOLIGAN. A magnificent prospect.

BERYL. Our garden is in a state as well, I'm afraid.

HOOLIGAN. Ah sure, it's a bit more civilized than the Congo at
any rate.

BERYL. Have you just arrived on our shores?

HOOLIGAN. Indeed, after ten years among the small tribes of
Africa.

BERYL. How exciting. I expect you'll find us a bit colourless after
that.

HOOLIGAN. Not at all.

BERYL. May I pour you a sherry?

HOOLIGAN. Well now, just a wee taste.

BERYL. Such a pity about your predecessor. A charming man.

HOOLIGAN. Charming to a fault.

BERYL. I do hope he and the late Mother Superior find happiness
in some distant place.

HOOLIGAN. I believe they're living in Kilburn. At any rate, he
had a great regard for you, Mrs Sedley. A fine woman and a
true Christian, those were his very words.

BERYL. That was kind of him. None of us is perfect, but I do try.

HOOLIGAN. A fine woman. Would you think me inquisitive if I
inquired is that a permanent arrangement you have there?

Indicates BERYL's *housecoat which has matting sewn into the front.*

BERYL. What must you think of me. It's my kneeling coat.

HOOLIGAN. That'd be some kind of matting.

BERYL. It's stitched in, you see.

HOOLIGAN. That's a remarkable idea.

BERYL. It's just that being a housewife and a Catholic I seem to spend such a time on my knees.

HOOLIGAN. Remarkable.

BERYL. As we're on the subject, Father. I dare say Father O'Connor forgot to mention but if you could call to the house in civilian attire. It's my husband, you see. He's got an attitude towards clergymen.

HOOLIGAN. Isn't that a terrible thing.

BERYL. It's that Sunday paper of his. They will give prominence to a certain kind of story. Father O'Connor's lapse from grace has only added fuel to the flames.

HOOLIGAN. Sure when a clergyman falls he comes down like an elephant, as they say. (*Finishes his drink*). Well, Mrs Sedley, I'll not delay the good news a moment longer. You'll be glad to hear the Parole Board have looked favourably on young Edward's application.

BERYL. Edward?

HOOLIGAN. I believe my predecessor mentioned the boy.

BERYL. I expect he may have. I'm afraid I don't recall. He had such penetrating eyes.

HOOLIGAN. Sure Edward's a grand lad. Not a scrap of harm in him. As they say in Ireland, if he had only one eye in the middle of his face you'd see the Star of Bethlehem shining out of it. He'll be no trouble.

BERYL. Trouble, Father?

HOOLIGAN. Edward's parole will be on condition we find him a place in a good Catholic home.

BERYL. You mean with us?

HOOLIGAN. I hardly think we need look any further for that.

BERYL. I don't know really. I shouldn't think George would approve.

HOOLIGAN. Only a couple of weeks. Till the papers are signed.

BERYL. We've got that asylum youth already. It's not as if we're shorthanded.

HOOLIGAN. A formality, as they say. Maybe you'd like to have a word with him first.

BERYL. I'm expecting Mr Sedley any minute.

HOOLIGAN. A more upright and manly fellow you never laid eyes on.

He crosses to the door and opens it. NED *is seated on the floor outside having a quiet smoke. He stubs it out and gets up.*

Would you step in a moment, Edward. I'd like you to say hallo to your employer.

NED. Nice to meet you, love.

BERYL. Edward, isn't it?

HOOLIGAN. Well, Edward. Answer me straight. What do you say to lending Mrs Sedley a hand about the house?

NED. Yeh, all right.

HOOLIGAN. There now, what did I tell you?

BERYL. It is good of you to offer. But as I was explaining to Father, the trouble is finding you something to do really.

HOOLIGAN. There's plenty to do in a house like this.

BERYL. We've got one retarded youth here already you see.

NED. How about a spot of decorating?

HOOLIGAN. Indeed, this room could do with a bit of a lick.

BERYL. I couldn't agree more, Father, only —

HOOLIGAN. Are you any sort of hand at it?

NED. Not much you could teach me about decorating.

HOOLIGAN. Is that so?

BERYL. It's my husband's room, you see.

NED. Knot, stopping, priming. Two coat emulsions.

HOOLIGAN. Do you hear that, Mrs Sedley?

NED. Polythene. Etylene. One coat lacquer.

HOOLIGAN. Sure he's a gift from Heaven itself. As they say don't turn away from Providence or it might jump up on your back.

BERYL. I should have to obtain Mr Sedley's consent.

HOOLIGAN. He'll give the furniture a going over as well. I'll tell
you, Mrs Sedley, he could turn this place into a palace.

BERYL. He's making it into a photographic studio.

HOOLIGAN. A photographic studio. Sure there's no end to the
possibilities. I'll leave you both to sort out the details. I have to
get started on an appeal for a pygmy cathedral in Africa.

BERYL. I'll just fetch my purse.

She goes off.

HOOLIGAN. Well, Edward, I trust you're sincere in your desire
for conversion.

NED. It's the Faith for me, Padre.

HOOLIGAN. This is the place to let it ripen and grow. In the
bosom of a family. That's a fine garden she has there. It'd be
a godsend for the Holy Sisters.

NED. I'll drop a few words in her ear.

HOOLIGAN. They're anxious to find space for a mortuary.

NED. Leave it with me.

BERYL *enters.*

BERYL. What a wonderful concept. A pygmy cathedral.

HOOLIGAN. Sure the poor divils are only so high. They need to
be reminded of bigger things. (*Extends a hand.*) Well, Mrs
Sedley, palace or photographic studio, you'll not be disappointed
with the results.

BERYL. It is thoughtful of you, Father, but I really don't —

HOOLIGAN. Edward, I know I'm leaving you in good hands.

NED. Thanks again, Padre.

HOOLIGAN. I'll see you both during Sunday Mass.

BERYL. I'll just see you out.

HOOLIGAN. Don't stir, Mrs Sedley. Sure, if I climbed up on the
shed there and on to the tree and took of a bit of a running
jump along that branch, with God's help I'd clear the barbed
wire and drop into the convent itself. Good day to you.

HOOLIGAN *goes off into the garden.*

BERYL. What a gallant soul.

NED. I could see he was somewhat attracted to you.

BERYL. Nonsense, dear. I'm sure he's got more important things on his mind. He does have a way with the ladies. Well, as you're here, Edward, I suppose I'd better find out a bit about you, if I may.

NED. Sure. Fire ahead.

BERYL. It's just I've got a young daughter in the house. I'd have to satisfy myself that you were fit company.

NED. What do you want to know?

BERYL. Father Hooligan did mention that you'd been granted some sort of reprieve. Was it a very serious charge?

NED. I'd call it a youthful indiscretion, really.

BERYL. Oh, that does sound a bit – nothing to do with sex, was it?

NED. Sex? Nothing like that. I had a slight altercation with the Law.

BERYL. What about?

NED. My beliefs.

BERYL. In Grosvenor Square, was it? You didn't strike one of our horses, did you?

NED. No, just a policeman. In the High Street.

BERYL. Our High Street?

NED. Outside Barclay's Bank. I'd gone in to get some money.

BERYL. And you hadn't anything in your account.

NED. I hadn't got an account.

BERYL. Where do your beliefs come into it?

NED. I'd formulated a theory that money ought to be freely available. On tap. As a reward for being born. Your birth certificate is your credit card.

BERYL. It does sound a trifle complicated.

NED. I was trying to simplify it when he started to thump me.

BERYL. Were you badly in need of the money?

NED. Halfway to desperate.

BERYL. I expect you needed a new bicycle.

NED. It was for a dear friend. She needed an operation.

BERYL. That was noble of you. Couldn't she get it under the Health Service?

NED. She was short of a number of stamps.

BERYL. Well, I'm so glad to hear there were extenuating circumstances. We've got so many nice things in our home.

NED. I should keep 'em locked up.

BERYL. I do dear. In my dressing-table. But don't tell Mr Sedley. He might be tempted to dispose of them.

NED. Shan't breathe a word.

BERYL. Now, about pocket money. If I were to engage you I expect you'd need some sort of financial reward. Or is that contrary to your beliefs?

NED. I could accept it under the heading of expenses.

BERYL. How much did they give you in prison?

NED. One and six a week.

BERYL. Oh dear, that's not very much. I expect we could manage a bit more.

NED. You're more than generous.

BERYL. Would two shillings be all right? It comes out of my housekeeping you see.

NED. Whatever you think.

BERYL. As to sleeping accommodation. We have a bed made up in the garage for Michael, so if you wouldn't mind sharing. The bathroom is at the top of the stairs. There is just one thing, Edward. Mr Sedley, I regret to say, has acquired the habit of using the flowerbed outside as a toilet, so you will avert your eyes if you have occasion to pass it.

SANDRA, *in school uniform, comes in with a variety of boxes and parcels.*

There you are, dear. Come and say hallo. We've got a young man coming to stay.

SANDRA (*hiding her face*). Don't look at me. (*She goes on out into the hall.*) Not now.

BERYL. She's at the awkward age. You won't go out of your way to tease, Edward. You never know when you're going to find they've put their head in a plastic bag.

NED. You can trust me.

BERYL. You've got uncommonly truthful eyes, Edward. Did you know that?

NED. It's been pointed out.

BERYL. What a blessing. If it's one thing I cannot abide, it's an untruth. I'll get you a garage key. (*She tugs at a drawer.*) This is my husband's part of the house really. He's in the Civil Service. He will have his own little kingdom. (*Tugs at the drawer.*) I'll get Michael to it. He's got a way with locks.

She goes out to the garden. NED *moves over to the silver cabinet. He takes up a teapot, and examines it.* MICK *enters.*

MICK. Got a match?

NED. Sure.

MICK. How about petrol?

NED. Eh?

MICK. Got any petrol hidden away?

NED. Sorry.

MICK. Go on. Search your pockets.

NED. Sorry. Right out.

MICK. Never nind. (*He wanders downstage.*) What I come in for?

NED. Drawer's stuck.

MICK. Make do with this. (*He takes a match, bites off the head, inserts it in the keyhole.*) Match. Pin. (*He takes a pin from his lapel.*) Excuse me. (*He takes off his boot.*) Stand back a bit.

NED *stands back.*

Right. (*He starts palming and stroking the head of the pin.*) Go on. Go on, boy. Hup? Go on now. Eh?

He brings the boot down smartly on the top. The drawer shoots out into his hands.

NED. How d'you do that?

MICK. Dunno, I got a gift.

NED. They teach you that somewhere?

MICK. No, I make it up as I go along.

NED. Could you show me?

MICK. I've forgotten already.

BERYL *comes in with blankets.*

BERYL. Has he opened it already? You are a clever fellow, aren't you? (*To* NED.) Your key, dear.

MICK. How about a reward?

BERYL. Oh, don't be silly. All right. Hands behind your back then.

MICK *puts his hands behind his back.* BERYL *presents her neck.* MICK *sinks a kiss into it.*

> That's enough, dear. (*To* NED.) He's got his funny little ways, our Michael. (*She goes on out into the hall.*)

MICK. What d'you think of her then?

NED. Eh?

MICK. All right, en't she?

NED. Not bad.

MICK. Eh? What d'you think?

NED. You bet.

MICK. En't she though. Eh? Coaarr!

NED. Coaarrr!

MICK *suddenly whips out a switchblade and applies it to* NED's *throat, bending him over backwards.*

MICK. Don't ever try it with her, mate.

NED. I wouldn't.

MICK. No?

NED. Honest.

MICK. Sure?

NED. I swear it.

MICK. Why not?

NED. What you mean?

MICK. What's the matter with her?

NED. Nothing.

MICK. You insinuating?

NED. Never.

MICK *shoves the knife back in his pocket.*

MICK. I take your word for it. (*He goes back, turns.*) Here. Who are you?

NED. I'm working here.

MICK. Funny we haven't met before.

NED. Only been here five minutes.

MICK. Keeping out of my way, are you?

NED. One minute.

MICK. Wouldn't lower yourself, is that it? (*He clicks open the knife, advances.*)

NED. Easy on, mate.

MICK. Mate? You a friend of mine or something?

NED. Yeh, don't you remember?

MICK. Sorry, chum, I get a bit mixed up. What's your name again?

NED. Ned.

MICK. Of course. (*Shakes hands.*) How do, Ned. Nice to see you again.

NED. And you.

MICK. You're looking well.

NED. Not so bad yourself.

MICK. Nice to see a familiar face.

NED. Brings you back.

MICK. Trouble is I'm practically certain I've never laid eyes on you, mate. What's your name again?

NED. Ned.

MICK. Pleased to meet you. (*Shakes hands.*) I'm . . . wassname.

NED. Michael?

MICK. That's it. How d'you know my name?

NED. We met before.

MICK. Yeh? What the bloody hell you keep shaking hands with me for then?

NED. I've been away.

MICK. Away? What you think this place is, a hotel?

SANDRA *comes in, transformed, with the help of a wig, long black dress, beads.*

How did you get out?

NED. I can't remember.

MICK. That's convenient. There's only one way out of this place, mate. Up.

NED. Yeh?

MICK. So how did you get out. Can you fly?

NED. No.

MICK. Neither can I. It's a bastard, en' it. (*Sees* SANDRA.) What do you think of her?

NED. What do I think of her?

MICK. Yeh.

NED. Yeh.

MICK. En't she?

NED. En't she though.

MICK. En't she what?

NED. What you just said.

MICK. What was that?

NED. En't she.

MICK. En't she though.

NED. I'll say.

MICK. Know something?

NED. What?

MICK. You're dead right, mate. Spot on. You describe her to perfection. The trouble is I couldn't give a monkey's one way or another. (*He moves away.*) I got a problem, see.

NED. What's that.

MICK. Dunno. I can't remember. That's the problem. I can't think what it is I've forgotten that I could be getting myself so steamed up about without being able to remember. (*He goes off into the garden.*)

SANDRA. He's a bit off.

NED. Really?

SANDRA. Up here.

NED. Can't say I noticed.

SANDRA. You must be worse than he is. D'you smoke it? (*She hands him a joint.*) You from the nuthouse too them?

NED. Not exactly.

SANDRA. No?

NED. Prison.

SANDRA. How long you in there?

NED. Six months.

SANDRA. Boy in our school just got ten years.

NED. What for?

SANDRA. Bored a hole through his Dad.

NED. What with?

SANDRA. Black and Decker.

NED. What did he do that for?

SANDRA. Just messing.

NED. Impressive.

SANDRA. He's only sixteen but ever so daring. How old are you?

NED. Twenty.

SANDRA. What you in for?

NED. Jumping the queue at Sainsbury's.

SANDRA. Not very exciting, is it?

NED. It's a start. Where d'you get this stuff?

SANDRA. Fella.

NED. Bit young for that kind of thing, en't you?

SANDRA. I'm older than him, he's only thirteen.

NED. Buys it up West, does he?

SANDRA. No, grows it in his desk at school. He's got everything. Pot, French Blues, Brown Bombers, Acid – makes it up with his Home Chemistry Set.

NED. Actually, I'm trying to get back on sweets.

SANDRA. I expect you thought I was just a child when I come through.

NED. The thought crossed my mind.

SANDRA. It's my Dad. He'd have a fit if he saw me like this. How old would you say I was? In this?

NED. Thirty-five.

SANDRA. Thirty-five? Do I look that old? That's a bit old, isn't it? How about if I take off the glasses?

NED. Eleven.

SANDRA. I want to look about nineteen.

NED. Take out one of the lenses.

SANDRA. Got no idea, have you?

NED. What age are you exactly?

SANDRA. Fifteen. But I've had a lot of experience.

NED. What sort of experience.

SANDRA. What do you think? You married?

NED. No.

SANDRA. Pity. You might have been able to teach me something. Not that I need much teaching. I've had just about everything. How about you?

NED. Nothing much. Luton Girls' Choir, Beverley Sisters. Usual thing.

SANDRA. Bit backward for twenty, are you?

NED. I'm a late developer.

SANDRA. How'd you like to take me out tonight?

NED. What for?

SANDRA. What d'you think?

NED. I'd have to consider it.

SANDRA. Why?

NED. I could be had for statutory rape.

SANDRA. What's that?

NED. A criminal offence.

SANDRA. Maybe you could teach me. Well? Don't think I'm mad about you or anything. I'd prefer Michael really. But he don't know what I'm on about. Thinks I want to set fire to his mattress or something. Right, I'll see you later. We can go out the back.

NED. Yeh?

SANDRA. Oh, I better warn you.

NED. What?

SANDRA. I don't kiss.

NED. No?

SANDRA. I can't be bothered.

NED. Past it, eh?

SANDRA. I don't want to get involved.

NED. You're safe with me.

SANDRA. You sure you're not from the nuthouse? Right, I'll see you later. I'll bring some pot. We can go in the toolshed.

NED. What do we do in there?

SANDRA. That's up to you, en' it?

BERYL *enters with a cardboard box.*

BERYL. Getting acquainted, you two? I thought you might like a game of Monopoly. You better get changed, dear. Whatever would your father think if he saw you like that!

SANDRA *goes off.* BERYL *sniffs.*

I've a suspicion she's having the odd Woodbine. You won't encourage her, Edward. At that age they just don't realize the necessity of lungs.

SEDLEY *backs in from the garden, buttoning his flies and carrying a large brown paper parcel.*

BERYL. Oh, did you have a nice day, dear?

SEDLEY. Eh? (*Tries to conceal the parcel.*) What are you doing down here?

BERYL. Nothing, dear.

SEDLEY. Got your own part of the house, haven't you?

BERYL. I was just on my way to the garden.

SEDLEY. What's wrong with the kitchen window, then? I've bought you a flight of steps. I paid three pound fifteen for those steps and there they are laying inutile under the stairs.

BERYL. Dear, I wish you wouldn't be so fussy. I was just showing Edward the lay of the land.

SEDLEY. Edward?

BERYL. Edward, dear. That young man over there.

SEDLEY *lifts his glasses.*

SEDLEY. That convent crowd been at you again. What's this then? Another one of their subhuman derelicts? (*He comes over.*) What's your affliction, son? What are you? Halfwit? Paralytic?

NED. Eh?

SEDLEY. Meths drinker? Say ah.

NED. Ah.

SEDLEY. That a real arm you got there or a mechanical substitute? (*He lifts* NED's *arm and lets it fall.*) Had a bloke here last week with great metal spikes sticking out of his wrists. Window cleaner he calls himself. Cuh! Damn near smashed every pane o' glass in the house. Finishes up falling through the French windows and impaling himself on the sofa. (*To* BERYL.) Well, what's he doing here?

BERYL. We thought perhaps, your room dear.

SEDLEY. What about my room?

BERYL. We thought you might like to have it decorated.

SEDLEY. My room. Do you mean to tell me that you have just engaged him to decorate my rom?

BERYL. Not exactly engaged, dear. It's just that it is getting a bit —

SEDLEY. I don't want it decorated, Beryl! I won't stand for it.

BERYL. Very well, dear.

SEDLEY. It is my room, Beryl!

BERYL. I do wish you wouldn't shout so. I mean, it is my house if it comes to that.

SEDLEY. Your house, is it? Well, let me tell you something. I have camped down here for fourteen years. Fourteen years, man and boy, I've had undisputed possession of this room. Why, Beryl?

BERYL. We've got a visitor, George.

SEDLEY. Because I've been establishing a right, that's why. I've got a statutory right to this room. Good as a freehold. Upheld in any court of Law.

BERYL. I don't see how that can be so.

SEDLEY. Permit me to understand an Englishman's heritage, Beryl. Now, if you please. (*He starts ushering her out.*) As the legal occupant I will deal with this.

BERYL. I'm sorry, Edward, you have to be humiliated.

SEDLEY. If you please. (*He shows her out and closes the door.*) Now, let's have this out. I believe my wife has engaged you to decorate my room?

NED. Correct.

SEDLEY. Do you have that in writing?

NED. No.

SEDLEY. Right. You can shove off back where you came from. You haven't a leg to stand on. I dare say you might recover your bus fare from a Lords' Tribunal. Take my advice you'll let the matter drop. And you can tell that crowd of vultures that any further intrusions will be dealt with in the same peremptory manner.

NED. What vultures?

SEDLEY. Come off it, son. I know who sent you. You're one of her lot, aren't you? That R.C. mob out the back.

NED. Who, me? Wouldn't touch it.

SEDLEY. No? How did you get mixed up with my wife then?

NED. We met through an intermediary.

SEDLEY. Who was that.

NED. Originally, it was Father O'Connor.

SEDLEY. What, from the convent?

NED. Correct.

SEDLEY. Who put Mother Superior up the spout?

NED. So I believe.

SEDLEY. What's that got to do with my wife?

NED. I'm a bank robber.

SEDLEY. I beg your pardon.

NED. A bank robber.

SEDLEY. I fail to see any connection.

NED. It's somewhat tortuous.

SEDLEY. I'm a Civil Servant, son. I live in an atmosphere of startling irrelevancy anyway. We'd got as far as Father O'Connor.

NED. He used to visit the prison.

SEDLEY. What for?

NED. Keep track of his flock. I met him in the canteen. It was Friday.

SEDLEY. Well?

NED. I happened to have chosen the fish course.

SEDLEY. On purpose.

NED. There was a certain amount of duplicity.

SEDLEY. He mistook you for one of his own.

NED. I allowed him to take me in hand.

SEDLEY. Compounding his original error.

NED. Persuade me of the necessity of living a better life.

SEDLEY. Outside the narrow confines.

NED. You seem to have got hold of the drift.

SEDLEY. Yes, it's practically identical to our method of obtaining a departmental transfer. In our case, we try to pose as Rotarians.

NED. Which brings me to here.

SEDLEY. Well, you seem capable of some initiative, son. Even if you are a criminal. It's not a quality you find at the top these days. I reckon we'd need men of the calibre of the Great Train robbers to sort out the Trade Unions.

NED. I've heard that said.

SEDLEY. Ex-prisoner, eh? I've got a certain interest in the seamy side of life.

NED. It has its fascination.

SEDLEY. I dare say it compensates for the unsmiling rectitude of a government department.

NED. It's understandable.

SEDLEY. Bank robber eh? Which bank?

NED. Barclay's.

SEDLEY. What, in the High Street?

NED. Two doors from Woolworths.

SEDLEY. It's a bit exposed. I wonder you didn't consider the Midland.

NED. Where's that?

SEDLEY. Round the corner, next door to the public lavatory.

NED. What, opposite the police station?

SEDLEY. You could have pulled the job, run down the steps, done some sort of quick change in cubicle and emerged as a West Indian bus conductor.

NED. That's quite a brilliantly conceived idea.

SEDLEY. Just speculating, son.

NED. Perhaps you're in the wrong profession.

SEDLEY. I dare say our approach to work is not dissimilar. Stealthy preparation, hasty execution and a quick exit from the scene of the crime to avoid retribution. Well, well, what an interesting life you must have.

NED. It has its moments.

SEDLEY. Yes, I can imagine. Pitting your wits against the vast apparatus of law and order . . . carrying it out against insurmountable odds . . . and then . . . alone . . . in some tiny room . . . with some bint who's as bent as you are . . . drunk with that matchless feeling of power . . . Let 'em all come . . . let 'em all . . .

BERYL *enters*. SEDLEY's *glasses fall off*.

What in hell do you want?

BERYL. Nothing. I just wondered how much longer you intended subjecting Edward to a tirade of abuse.

SEDLEY. Tirade of abuse? Whatever are you talking about, Beryl? This young man and I happen to be in the throes of a business discussion.

BERYL. Is that true, Edward?

SEDLEY. Of course it's true.

BERYL. He's not been saying horrible things, has he?

SEDLEY. What a funny person you are, Beryl. Really, what an incredible person you are.

BERYL. All right, George. There's no need to be abusive.

SEDLEY. Abusive, my love? A moment ago you accused me of abusing him. Now, apparently, I'm abusing you; it looks to me as if you've got abusing on the brain, my love.

BERYL. Very well, George.

SEDLEY. You're abuse fixated, if you ask me.

BERYL. Anything you say, dear. (*She goes off.*)

SEDLEY. Abusive? Well I never. My word. You married?

NED. No.

SEDLEY. You're better off in a Maximum Security Wing. Can't think what came over me to marry something like that. It was during the war, of course. They'd conditioned you to accept all kinds of tasteless substitutes. Used to visit her on leave. God knows why. Not even the abandonments of VE day could tempt our Beryl from the paths of virtue. I hoped she might surrender along with the Germans. In fact, she held out six days longer than the Japanese. Yes, that's what it took to get her on her back. Global conflict, Europe in ruins, nine million dead and two Atom bombs. They might have saved themselves the trouble. Forgive me if I reminisce.

NED. I find it fascinating. A little fragment of military history.

SEDLEY. Yes, we've arrived at a stalemate. Done everything short of digging trenches and erecting the barbed wire. Well, well, so you thought of doing a spot of decorating, did you?

NED. With your permission.

SEDLEY. I thought of converting this room into a photographic studio.

NED. I'd be happy to oblige.

SEDLEY. I've got plans for this house. If some pack of clergymen don't get their hands on it. (*Gazes out.*) Look where I'm placed. Convent down the end, Vicarage next door. If this Church unity thing goes through I'll be wiped off the map. They're after my garden.

NED. I wouldn't credit it.

SEDLEY. Want to extend their cemeteries. Packed tight. Putting them in head first as far as I can make out. Be shoving them under my wall next, I shouldn't wonder. (*He moves away.*) Well, I'm not a man for firm commitments, son. Let's say you're engaged on a trial basis to expire at some unspecified future date. How much she paying you again?

NED. Four shillings a week.

SEDLEY. I'll raise it to four and six. Then you'll know where your allegiance lies. Put you in the garage?

NED. I believe so.

SEDLEY. I won't hear of it. Kip down here if you like. Nice view. Convent dormitory just over the way. Got a four-inch telescope in there if you're interested. Dare say that wouldn't appeal to a lad of your calibre. Got bigger things in hand, eh?

NED. Here and there.

SEDLEY. Yes, well I'm prepared to tolerate your presence here,

son. You've got some sort of red blood in your veins at any
rate. I'd best sort out my wife on the subject.

SEDLEY *goes out into the hall.* SANDRA *enters.*

NED. Nice parents you got.

SANDRA. Yeh. They've got a big love scene going.

NED. Kipping in there with his telescope. What's your Mum
do for it?

SANDRA. She reads *Gone with the Wind* in bed every night.

NED. It's like home.

SANDRA. You coming?

NED. Bit nippy out there.

SANDRA. Suit yourself. I've brought some pot.

NED. Ta.

SANDRA. Thirty bob's worth.

NED. Got any money?

SANDRA. Yeah lots.

NED. Lend us thirty bob.

SANDRA. Why, you skint?

NED. I'll pay you the end of the week.

SANDRA. D'you want to make some real money?

NED. How?

SANDRA. On the side.

NED. What would I have to do?

SANDRA. It's my secret. Promise you won't tell anyone.

NED. What?

SANDRA. I'm not a schoolgirl.

NED. You're an old age pensioner.

SANDRA. No, I'm a criminal.

NED. Go on.

SANDRA. I've got a gang. We're all over the newspapers. Read
it.

She hands him a tiny newspaper clipping.

NED. Read it? I can hardly see it.

SANDRA. Go on.

NED. 'Coinbox vandals need horsewhipping says councillor.'
That's you, is it?

SANDRA. Us.

NED. How many in the gang?

SANDRA. Two.

NED. You and who else?

SANDRA. Michael.

NED. An unbeatable combination. Hopelessly immature and down-right thick. You'll make a fortune.

SANDRA. We're thinking of moving into something bigger.

NED. What, weighing machines?

SANDRA. Dunno yet. We could do with some extra help. Well?

NED. What's it worth?

SANDRA. A quarter share.

NED. How much does that work out in sixpences?

SANDRA. Fifty-fifty then?

NED. Do me a favour.

SANDRA. Too risky.

NED. Far too risky.

SANDRA. Scared?

NED. Yeh, terrified.

SANDRA. I'm not afraid.

NED. You've got the joy of probation to look forward to. I get back in, I'm in there for keeps. Leading a bunch of kids astray. They'd crucify me.

SANDRA. I thought you might like some experience.

NED. I don't need experience. I'm a professional.

SANDRA. I thought you did something in Tesco.

NED. No, I'm a bank man, love. One bank, three post offices, two sweetshops.

SANDRA. You're just what we're looking for.

NED. You're not what I'm looking for. I'm here for a rest. A little bit of a relax before going up West and getting into the big time. Anyway, leading that thundering great ape around. It's impossible.

SANDRA. He can get anything open.

NED. Can he keep anything shut?

SANDRA. I'd let you kiss me.

NED. I don't kiss.

SANDRA. Neither do I. We could get on terrific. We're going on a job tonight. Want to come?

NED. Sorry, love. I don't work for peanuts.

SANDRA. Right. Could I have my thirty bob then?

NED. I'll give you a cheque. (*He takes out a cheque book.*)

SANDRA. Got identification?

NED. I'm a professional, love. I don't walk about with a pocketful of giveaways.

SANDRA. What's your name?

NED. Edward R. Betts, Esq.

SANDRA. Got it written down anywhere?

NED. No.

SANDRA. Sorry, too risky.

NED. Apart from my tattoo.

SANDRA. Tattoo?

NED. I've got it tattooed on my stomach.

SANDRA. What for?

NED. If they get that far, I'd prefer to tell all.

SANDRA. Can I have a look?

NED. Trusting soul, aren't you?

He lifts up his shirt, rolls down his pants top, and bares his stomach.

SANDRA. It's a bit illegible.

NED. It could do with a retouch.

SANDRA. Spreading a bit.

NED. I'm making room for my middle initial. Satisfied?

SANDRA. How do I know if it's yours?

NED. All right, I'll come clean. I borrowed the stomach for the evening. My real name is underneath. Farther down. I show it to lady bank cashiers and when they faint and fall over, I rifle the till. That is why the level of a bank counter gets that little bit higher every year.

SEDLEY *enters.*

> And that is why when two lady bank cashiers get together they will converse in shuddering whispers about the gentleman known as . . . The Flash.

He becomes aware of SEDLEY. *He quickly pulls down his shirt.* SANDRA *turns away and goes out into the garden.*

NED. Just getting acquainted.

SEDLEY. So I notice. Interesting girl.

NED. Yes.

SEDLEY. From around these parts?

NED. I believe so.

SEDLEY. She's got a familiar look about her. Known each other long?

NED. No, we've just met.

SEDLEY. Don't waste much time, do you? My word. In my day, before you get that far, you'd need an engagement ring, wedding ring, a thirty-year mortgage on your back and even then it took place in pitch darkness.

NED. Changing times.

SEDLEY. Dare say you've got quite a few little friends like that?

NED. Dozens.

SEDLEY. That's the spirit. Might as well enjoy yourself while you're young. If you attempt it in later life you'll find it's liable to some sort of criminal prosecution. The fact is, you may be able to do something for me.

NED. What's that?

SEDLEY. It's to do with my photography really. I'm quite a keen photographer. (*He takes up the brown paper parcel.*) Anyone out the back?

NED. No.

SEDLEY *tears off the paper to reveal a lifesize shop dummy with one leg missing.*

SEDLEY. What do you think of that, then?

NED. Magnificent.

SEDLEY. Not bad, is it? Found it abandoned in the High Street. I specialize in the human figure, you see. The trouble is I'm having difficulty in finding suitably live subjects.

NED. I can well believe it.

SEDLEY. So when I see a keen young type like yourself, I say to myself . . .

NED. You want me . . .

SEDLEY. How shall I put it . . .

NED. . . . to peel off, is that it?

SEDLEY. You? My word, not you, son. What do you think I am, some kind of pervert? No, perhaps you might have some little lady friend who'd care to earn a few shillings modelling now and then.

NED. I could have a look around.

SEDLEY. Perfectly straightforward. I'm hoping to do a whole series of photographs under some such title as the Dawn of Woman.

NED. It's a good title.

SEDLEY. Yes, it may give you a clue as to what is required.

NED. Clue?

SEDLEY. The young lady should represent early morning. I mean it's no use coming up with some bint who looks like the last stroke of midnight.

NED. I'll have a scrape around.

SEDLEY. You'll bear in mind that as a servant of Her Majesty I've got a position to uphold. Discreet inquiries you understand.

NED. No names.

SEDLEY. Or addresses. You may well care to bring her here in a blindfold or something. I leave it to your discretion.

NED. I'll think of something.

SEDLEY. Yes, well, I dare say we shall get along reasonably well together, son. If there's one thing I might request, it's that you, let us say, steer clear of my young daughter. She's been quietly brought up. Rose hip syrup, 'Jackanory'. I'm anxious to protect her from the seamy side of life.

The door opens. BERYL *remains outside as* SANDRA *enters in a dressing-gown.*

BERYL. Say goodnight to your father, dear.

SEDLEY. Hello, my little dumpling. I haven't seen you all day now have I?

SANDRA. No, Dad.

SEDLEY. Give old Bumble Bear his kiss then.

SANDRA *gives him a peck.*

SANDRA. G'night, Dad.

SEDLEY. Goodnight, my sweet darling. Be sure and pull your curtains when you go up. Never know what foul-minded swine is lurking outside in search of lewd gratification. Leaving your window open?

SANDRA. Expect so.

SEDLEY (*opens a drawer*). Better have my service revolver then. And remember, if any bloke tries to climb in your window, even if it's the vicar, let him have it, preferably in the lower half of the stomach. I'll load it for you.

SANDRA. Should I kiss him too, Dad?

SEDLEY. I don't see why not, my love.

SANDRA *tries to kiss* NED. NED *avoids it.* SANDRA *pulls out his shirt.*

There we are.

NED *tucks in his shirt.* SANDRA *takes a poke.*

All cocked up and ready to shoot, eh?

NED. Eh?

SANDRA (*taking the revolver*). G'night, Dad.

SEDLEY. Goodnight, my love.

SANDRA *goes off.*

Sweet lovely girl. She's the one decent thing left in this sink of corruption. I'd strangle any man as much as laid a hand on her. Tear him apart with my bare hands. You may not be aware, son, but there's a type of bloke who takes an unhealthy interest in young ladies. I've got simple and direct views on that type of individual.

NED. What would you recommend?

SEDLEY. I reckon they ought to be debollocked.

NED. Publicly?

SEDLEY. Trafalgar Square would be the place. They could erect some huge hydraulic appliance. A cross between a guillotine and a giant bottle opener. Well, might as well turn in, I suppose. (*He hovers around the window.*) Not a bad night, Friday. Yes, it's surprising what night skies doth betimes reveal. I'll say goodnight.

NED. Goodnight, Mr Sedley. You got a nice family. It's something of the home I always dreamed about but never had.

SEDLEY. I dare say we're no worse than most, son. (*He starts to go in, pauses.*) Oh, just one thing. I'd keep clear of that flowerbed outside the door if I were you. Never know what sort of verminous rubbish that woman is going to leave laying about. (*He goes into the study.*)

BERYL *enters with a rug and pillow.*

BERYL. Has Mr Sedley retired for the evening?

NED. I believe so.

BERYL. I expect he's busy with one of his hobbies. Well, Edward, it is nice to have you with us for a bit. I do hope you're not bored out of your mind as our daughter would say. As you can see we're just ordinary people really.

NED. It's a pleasant change.

BERYL. Do you have difficulty in getting off to sleep?

NED. Only when there's something on my conscience.

BERYL. Well, I've brought you a copy of *Gone with the Wind* just in case.

NED. Thoughtful of you.

BERYL. I find it puts me right off.

MICK *enters.*

Goodnight, Edward.

BERYL *goes off.*

MICK. Coming on the work party then?

NED. What work party?

MICK. Smashing things open, ripping 'em apart.

NED. No. I'm staying in tonight.

MICK. In? What do you think this place is – a hotel?

SANDRA *enters.*

SANDRA. Coming then?

MICK. Course he's coming. Stick close together else they send the
    dogs after you. Shh! (*He stiffens.*) They're blowing the whistle.

SANDRA. He thinks it's a nuthouse.

NED. Does he?

MICK. Come on.

They go out into the garden.

CURTAIN

ACT TWO

Three weeks later.
The room is repainted. There are two stepladders spanned by planks
adjoining the study door. NED *is lying back on the planks, bare*
chested, with SANDRA *partly covered by a dustsheet, smoking.*
SEDLEY *enters, carrying a parcel.* NED *sits up.* SANDRA *ducks down.*

NED. Back early, Mr S.

SEDLEY. Come down here a minute.

He goes out through the windows. NED *slips on his trousers and*
follows.

Well?

NED. What?

SEDLEY. I think I'm entitled to an explanation.

NED. Where?

SEDLEY. There.

NED. What are they?

SEDLEY. Come off it, son. You know damn well what they are.
They're some sort of contraceptive device. What they doing in
the flowerbed?

NED. I can't imagine.

SEDLEY. What's going on? It's like some sort of floral family
planning clinic. Where'd they come from?

NED. Maybe those tower blocks.

SEDLEY. What tower blocks?

NED. Over there.

SEDLEY. They're about three miles away, son. I can't think what
fit of communal abandon could propel them that distance.

NED. Maybe they fell from an aeroplane.

SEDLEY. Yes, and maybe you've been having that bint of yours
round here every night for a fortnight. It's too much, son. I
employed you as a decorator, not a blood stallion. I've got a sensi-

tive child sleeping overhead. You'd best pack up your things as soon as that wall's dried out. I take it it has dried out by now.

NED. Still a bit tacky.

SEDLEY. It was tacky yesterday.

NED. I gave it another coat.

SEDLEY. What are you trying to do – pauperize me? You've spent three weeks here flinging paint around like Michelangelo. I'm out there labouring like a swineherd.

NED. I can promise the room for this evening.

SEDLEY. You promised something else for this evening. That model of yours.

NED. She got held up. Expect her tomorrow.

SEDLEY. I expected her yesterday.

NED. Nothing like the pleasures of anticipation.

SEDLEY. After three weeks of waiting, son the pleasure is beginning to harden into sheer, boneshaking fantasy.

NED. I'll give her a ring.

SEDLEY. What's her name again?

NED. Georgina.

SEDLEY. I thought it was Maxine.

NED. She changes her name about. Professional reasons.

SEDLEY. Well as long as she doesn't change her sex about for professional reasons. (*He unwraps the parcel, disclosing a plaster leg.*) I'm beginning to think she's a figment of your imagination. I've spent most of my life chasing figments already. I could do with a spot of reality. (*He fits the leg to the dummy. Too short.*) God's teeth, look at that, eh?

NED. Not exactly Miss Universe, no.

SEDLEY. What a sorry mess of a country. Why can't they make one thing to standard size? You break a leg, you throw it away.

NED. It's as bad as the Health Service.

SEDLEY. I shall have to make other use of my equipment.

NED. Going out?

SEDLEY (*packs up his camera and tripod*). Yes, I'm falling back on an alternative. Keep an eye to doors and windows when I'm gone. That teenage gang may be rampaging about.

NED. Yes. I'll watch that for you.

SEDLEY. They're all over the papers again. Nicked the convent last night. Got away with a safe.

NED. Is that a fact?

SEDLEY. I'd give them the Duke of Edinburgh award. Friends of yours?

NED. I've no idea.

SEDLEY. Hm, I wonder. There's more to you than meets the eye, son. Hanging about week after week like a parasite.

NED. I like the quiet life.

SEDLEY. You got a fair share of brain. You could aspire to a junior clerical post.

NED. I couldn't take the responsibility.

SEDLEY. Yes, I dare say you've got more important things in hand.

NED. Police come up with anything?

SEDLEY. You'd best read it yourself, son. If you ask my candid opinion I'd say the Vicar is behind it. He's behind most things in these parts, not least his bevy of choirboys. I must be off. Show begins at eight o'clock.

NED. Pictures?

SEDLEY. No, the Girl Guide gymnastic display at the Drill Hall. It's about the nearest thing we've got to an all night Striporama around these parts.

NED. Don't get arrested.

SEDLEY. Some hope.

SEDLEY *goes off.* SANDRA *comes out from under the dustsheet.*

SANDRA. He'd kill me if he found out.

NED. What about me? I'm walking a tightrope these past few weeks. Days and nights of deceit. It's nerve-racking. I'd be better off in a trade.

SANDRA. You're not up to a life of crime.

NED. Crime? One daft schoolgirl. One halfwit. I'd be the laughing stock of the prison if they knew what I was into. I promised them a post office job, not a midnight stakeout with the Sisters of Mercy.

SANDRA. We're rich.

NED. Scrapings.

SANDRA. We've got hundreds.

NED. Do better on Supplementary Benefit.

SANDRA. Maybe they'll write a film about us.

NED. Yeh. Einstein's mob. Everything we do has got his big feet stamped all over it. Look at the headline. Vandals raid convent. I'm not a vandal, I'm a craftsman. What's he doing out there, a spot of brain surgery?

SANDRA. He's trying to open the safe.

NED. What's he done, run out of matches?

SANDRA. No, he's chatting it up.

NED. Chatting it up. That's all I need. To get nicked for a spot of safe chatting. Soon as I get out of here I'm going for a jackpot.

SANDRA. When you leaving?

NED. Immediately.

SANDRA. I shan't miss you.

NED. Messing with kids in a place like this. I need room to move. Light and air. Space. I ought to be up the West End not ferreting around the back end of nowhere.

BERYL's *head comes around the door.*

BERYL. Is he gone, dear?

NED. All clear.

BERYL (*entering*). What a blessed relief! I'm so weary of that eternal scullery.

NED. Relax, Mum. He's hit the trail.

BERYL (*to* SANDRA). Haven't you got your cardigan on, dear. You'll catch your death. Whatever are you doing there?

NED (*diverting*). You've had your hair done.

BERYL. Oh, you've noticed.

NED. Let's have a look. Hurry up.

SANDRA. Where are they?

NED (*turns her around*). You're a smasher. You'll be turning on
Father Hooligan.

SANDRA *is getting dressed.*

BERYL. Oh, go on with you.

NED. Filling his head with unchristian thoughts.

BERYL. You are a caution, Edward.

NED. He'll emulate his predecessor . . .

BERYL. Now, you're making fun of me, aren't you?

NED. No, I'm serious. He thinks you're stunning. Told me so
himself.

BERYL. Really? He does have a way with the ladies.

NED. You ought to elope together. Be a treat for the Sundays.

BERYL. I'm much too quiet to elope with anyone. I'm more of a
Gone with the Wind type, really.

NED. That's a pretty risky book, isn't it?

BERYL. On the contrary, Edward. It's the most beautiful story
ever told. I've read it every night since I was a girl.

NED. How about on your honeymoon?

BERYL. Even then. George was furious. He'd brought the literature of a more instructional nature.

NED. He would.

BERYL *sees* SANDRA'S *panties on the floor.*

BERYL. Sandra, whatever will Edward think of you. You're a big
girl now.

NED. I've got a kid sister of my own, Mrs S.

BERYL. You've been more than a brother to her, Edward. How we
shall manage when you're gone I don't quite know. You brought
an air of romance into our lives.

NED. Maybe we can all elope. The three of us and Father H.

BERYL. I expect he has other things on his mind, poor man. His
money stolen under the cloak of night. Young people nowa-
days, wherever do they get such dreadful ideas? It was all ping
pong and hiking in my day. What a blessing you're on the right
road, Edward.

NED. I've seen the light.

BERYL. I know. It's in your eyes dear. I knew it the very minute, you walked inside that door.

The door opens. MICK *comes in with the safe.*

MICK. OK, Chief. Where d'you want it?

NED. Not now.

BERYL. Michael, what sort of rubbish have you got there?

MICK. Where to, Chief?

BERYL. Take it out at once.

MICK. In or out?

NED. Better take it out.

MICK. You just said bring it in.

NED. Now I want it out.

MICK. Why?

NED. I don't want it now.

MICK. You don't want it?

NED. No thanks.

MICK. Sure about that?

NED. Definite.

MICK. Made up your mind have you?

NED. Near enough.

MICK. Tell me something. (*Comes up close.*) What have I been breaking my arse for all day then?

NED. I don't know.

MICK. He don't know.

NED. I don't know what I want.

MICK. You want slitting up the windpipe, that's what you want. Eight hours I spent. (*He holds up two fingers.*) It's got tumblers, see. They need chatting up.

BERYL. Tumblers, dear?

NED. It's a cocktail cabinet.

MICK. A what?

BERYL. We're not a drinking family. Throw it away.

NED. Take it outside.

MICK. What about the money?

BERYL. Money, dear?

MICK. There's money in it.

NED. What, that? Wouldn't get tuppence for it.

MICK. Eh?

NED. Second hand. (*Kicks it.*) It's got woodworm.

MICK. Woodworm. (*Kicks it.*) That's cast iron, mate.

BERYL. It is an odd contraption. Wherever did you find it?

SANDRA *interposes.*

SANDRA. Could I have a biscuit, Mum?

BERYL. Yes, of course, dear.

SANDRA. I like your hair.

BERYL. Do you?

SANDRA. It's beautiful.

NED. How about a cup of tea, love?

BERYL. In a moment.

SANDRA. Could I have cheese on it, Mum?

NED. Two lumps for me, please.

BERYL. Dear, I haven't got forty pairs of hands you know.

MICK. Here, what about me?

BERYL. Honestly, you children will be the death of me.

BERYL *goes off.*

SANDRA. What you keep turning her on to Father Hooligan for?

MICK. Out, you said.

NED. No, in, leave it.

MICK. Leave it. In. Out. They'll clap a jacket on you one of these
days.

NED. Christ, what I have to contend with, eh? Big mouth, big
feet. It's like training a load of circus animals to rob the Bank
of England.

MICK. I don't get it.

NED. You don't have it.

MICK. You're a bit loose in the tongue today. They'll be putting
clappers on your head if you're not careful.

NED. You want to chat it up a bit more?

MICK. No, they're asleep.

NED. What?

MICK. The tumblers. They're flogged out.

NED. They got my sympathy.

MICK. Watch it.

SANDRA. Here. Do that other thing you can do.

MICK. What other thing? Oh that. What other thing?

SANDRA. You know.

MICK. Ah.

He whispers to the safe. It comes apart. NED *takes out a bundle of notes.*

NED. Tenners.

SANDRA. How much?

NED. Maybe a thousand.

SANDRA. It's a fortune.

NED. I'd prefer a credit card.

SANDRA. We're rich.

NED. A little respite from daily toil. Bloody bits of paper. Why can't you sign a form for it?

SANDRA. I'm not listening.

NED. No, you're watching.

SANDRA. Half and half.

NED. That's about it.

MICK. What about me?

NED *peels off a note.*

NED. You been a big help.

MICK. Thanks. (*He looks at it.*) Who's she?

NED. Your Mum.

MICK. Thought I'd seen her before somewhere.

SANDRA. I want it counted.

NED. No time. Get rid of that.

SANDRA. How do I know if it's right?

NED. We send a statement at the end of the month.

SANDRA. I'm not having it.

NED. Well, open a Giro account then.

MICK. I want this counted.

SANDRA. You're cheating me.

NED. Look, what would I be doing chiselling a schoolgirl? I've just robbed a crowd of old nuns, that's bad enough. I'll be forging Welfare Milk tokens if it goes on like this.

BERYL *at the door.*

BERYL. Tea's in the kitchen, children. Whatever are you doing?
NED. Just playing.
SANDRA. Cops and robbers.
BERYL. All that money.
NED. It's Monopoly money.
BERYL. It's so real.
NED. It's a bank.
MICK. That's a safe.
NED. I'm a cashier.
SANDRA. I'm a bank robber.
HOOLIGAN (*off*). Are you there, Edward?
BERYL. Father Hooligan. It's in such a state.

BERYL *grabs a dustsheet and covers the safe.*

NED. Ta.
SANDRA. Thanks, Mum.

BERYL *goes out.*
Enter FATHER HOOLIGAN *in plain clothes.*

HOOLIGAN. Well, Edward, is it yourself?
NED. Evening, Padre.
HOOLIGAN. The Lord's blessing on the young people.
MICK. One of them, eh?
HOOLIGAN. And how's the fair Miss Sedley?
SANDRA. Middling.
HOOLIGAN. And who have we got here at all?
MICK. I don't know, mate. Got no idea.
HOOLIGAN. How's the wee maneen?
MICK. What's a wee maneen?
HOOLIGAN. How are we today?
MICK (*looking around*). I don't know, how are we today?
HOOLIGAN. How are we, at all?

MICK. Who's we, mate? What you keep saying we for?

HOOLIGAN. At all, at all.

MICK. There's only one of me, mate.

HOOLIGAN *turns away*.

HOOLIGAN. Ah, sure he's only a whim of Providence.

MICK. You meet 'em, don't you.

He goes out after SANDRA.

HOOLIGAN. Well, you seem happily installed here, Edward.

NED. It's been a wonderful experience, Father.

HOOLIGAN. Sure there's nothing like family life for bringing a lad down to earth. You may be sure if the Lord came down again he'd choose a home like this in preference to any number of Hilton Intercontinentals. Are you finished up yet?

NED. Near enough.

HOOLIGAN. That's good. You'll be glad to hear the Parole Board has put your case entirely in my hands.

NED. That's heartening news indeed.

HOOLIGAN. Have you had any thoughts about the future?

NED. You could say I'm entrusting myself to Providence.

HOOLIGAN. That's always a wise move. But I was thinking of something a bit more practical. Have you ever considered gravedigging as a possible career?

NED. It's a good bit down on my list.

HOOLIGAN. The poor devil we had in the cemetery sat down yesterday for a quiet lunch and a forty-foot mausoleum fell in on top of him. The Lord have mercy, but there's a job going if you're interested.

NED. I'd have to think a bit about it.

HOOLIGAN. A grand job. Four pounds a week and the protective clothing. We've a queue of applicants.

NED. It's worth considering.

HOOLIGAN. I hope you won't be too long about deciding to accept or we might have to return you to the authorities. As you can imagine we're not too kindly disposed towards desperadoes after the events of last night.

NED. I was shocked and saddened by the news, Father.

HOOLIGAN. We must accept it patiently as the will of Heaven and God help the culprits if ever I catch up with them. And now tell me how we're progressing with the other little matter.

NED. Matter?

HOOLIGAN. The matter of the garden.

NED. What garden?

HOOLIGAN. Name of God, have you no head on your shoulders at all. The garden out the back there. Haven't you spoken to Mrs Sedley about it? Haven't I the Holy Sisters pestering me about it for a week? Doesn't your liberty depend on it?

NED. Broadly speaking, it's in the bag.

HOOLIGAN. You've discussed it with her, then?

NED. Every night.

HOOLIGAN. That's good. Between ourselves, I believe the Vicar is desperate to get hold of it as well. We wouldn't want to be beaten to it by the other crowd. So she's favourable?

NED. Might take a little more persuading. It's her husband. He's got an aversion to clergymen.

HOOLIGAN. So it's just a question of persuading the husband. Tell me, what kind of man would he be?

NED. Mr Sedley? Average. Walk down any street.

HOOLIGAN. Does he have any religious leanings?

NED. I'd describe him as a freethinker.

HOOLIGAN. How free?

NED. Unbridled.

HOOLIGAN. Does he have any conception of the Universe?

NED. I've heard him describe it as a snakepit.

HOOLIGAN. That's a start. How about the human race?

NED. Moles ferreting in a dungheap.

HOOLIGAN. Sure we're halfway there. Who could think up a combination like that, only the Almighty Himself?

NED. That's a good point.

HOOLIGAN. You might care to mention it the next time you discuss the meaning of existence.

NED. I'll see if I can slip it in.

HOOLIGAN. I'm happy to see you've put your time to such good use here, Edward. You've done a fine job. (*He surveys the room.*) A photographic studio, eh? Sure it's fit for Lord Snowdon himself and he connected to the Blood Royal as they say. I suppose photography is an expensive undertaking. What's that piece of equipment there?

NED. There?

HOOLIGAN. Under the dustsheet. Is it a developing tank?

He goes over. NED *interposes.*

NED. It's personal actually.

HOOLIGAN. A personal developing tank.

NED. You could call it a shrine.

HOOLIGAN. A shrine?

NED. I carry it about with me in case I feel like a spot of worship.

HOOLIGAN. That's a terrible idea. No wonder the churches are half empty with these do-it-yourself worshipping kits. What's inside of it?

NED. Cherished possessions. They're sacred to me.

HOOLIGAN. Has it been blessed?

NED. Several times.

HOOLIGAN. Who by?

NED. His Highness the Pope.

HOOLIGAN. What, in Rome?

NED. No, on television. I stood it in front of the 'Sunday Break'.

HOOLIGAN. That's highly irregular.

NED. I'm a bit unorthodox.

BERYL *enters.*

HOOLIGAN. I think you need a longer period of instruction before you're ready for the Faith.

BERYL. Your tea is in the kitchen, Edward.

HOOLIGAN. Ah, Mrs Sedley. We'll discuss it at some later stage.

BERYL. Run along now.

NED *goes off.*

HOOLIGAN. Mrs Sedley. You're like a breath of fresh Spring air. A different outfit for each day of the week.

BERYL. It's good of you to notice in your hour of trial, Father. May I persuade you to a sherry?

HOOLIGAN. It'll help to refresh the drooping spirit.

BERYL. I'm sure we shan't sleep until the culprits have been brought to justice.

HOOLIGAN. A terrible business. The poor Sisters haven't got over it yet. A group of agile young men prowling the dormitories. God knows what might have happened. Half of them are still in a state of trance.

BERYL. All that money squandered on ice creams.

HOOLIGAN. Close on a thousand pounds.

BERYL. I expect you've had to abandon your pygmy cathedral.

HOOLIGAN. A great blow to my hopes. But as one project fades away, perhaps another pops up its head over the horizon which brings me to the purpose of my visit. (*Confidentially.*) You might as well know, Mrs Sedley, I'm here on a somewhat delicate matter.

BERYL. A delicate matter, Father?

HOOLIGAN. We must approach it by degrees for fear of treading on any corns. This is very much in the nature of a preliminary overture?

BERYL. Overture?

HOOLIGAN. Nevertheless I believe Edward may have dropped a few words in your ear over the past few weeks. Is that not so?

BERYL. Well, that is, he has made some observations of a bantering nature but of course it never occurred to me to think that he was serious.

HOOLIGAN. Oh, he was perfectly serious.

BERYL. Really?

HOOLIGAN. You might say I've employed him as a go-between.

BERYL. I'm sure I don't quite know what to say.

HOOLIGAN. Then you may have a general idea about what I'm after.

BERYL. I suppose so. In a way.

HOOLIGAN. May I take it that you're not averse to the idea?

BERYL. I haven't really thought about it.

HOOLIGAN. Sure take your time. There's no rush. As they say in Ireland, never force a lady's hand or you might get the other one smack in the teeth.

BERYL. I'm sure I've no such idea.

HOOLIGAN. I know you must have a few reservations. Connected with your husband.

BERYL. There is that, I suppose.

HOOLIGAN. You'd be worried about straining the marriage bond.

BERYL. I'm not sure it hasn't snapped. There is the question of right and wrong.

HOOLIGAN. Sure can it ever be wrong to give, Mrs Sedley? To give wholeheartedly and without restraint? To lay it at the feet of something greater than ourselves? May I expect a tentative yes?

BERYL. What is your first name, dear?

HOOLIGAN. Benedict. Why do you ask?

BERYL. I dare say I'm old fashioned but it does help to have a name to fall back on. I'm Beryl.

HOOLIGAN. How do you do, Beryl.

BERYL. Hello, Benedict.

HOOLIGAN. Then it's settled.

BERYL. I'm so undecided. Give me time.

HOOLIGAN. You'll never regret it. I promise you that.

BERYL. I'm such a *Gone with the Wind* person, you see.

HOOLIGAN. *Gone with the Wind?*

BERYL. It's always been up in my head. It's so difficult to make it come real.

HOOLIGAN. Have you been considering it for some time?

BERYL. I suppose I have been waiting for someone to come along.

HOOLIGAN. Sure what a blessing I turned up. You might never have got round to it. I take it there's no question of payment, then.

BERYL. I'm sure it would never enter my mind.

HOOLIGAN. I can promise you that the gift is accepted in the spirit in which it is given. Good. Let's have a drink on it.

BERYL. I expect it'll go straight to my head.

HOOLIGAN. From the head to the heart and thence to the open hand as they say.

BERYL. I suppose it is something of an occasion.

They pour drinks.

HOOLIGAN. Your health, Mrs Sedley.

BERYL. Beryl.

HOOLIGAN. Your health, Beryl.

BERYL. And you, Benedict.

HOOLIGAN. You've taken a great weight off my mind. The Mother Superior has been pestering me for weeks.

BERYL. Really?

HOOLIGAN. She's a devil of a woman when she gets going. At it night and day. Never leaves off. I'm destroyed with it.

BERYL. What a trial for you.

HOOLIGAN. You've made me a happy man. To tell you the truth I was afraid the Vicar might get in there first. Sure there's not a more attractive proposition in the neighbourhood.

BERYL. Thank you, dearest. (*She spills her drink.*)

HOOLIGAN. I've got great plans, Beryl.

BERYL. Tell me.

HOOLIGAN. I can't wait to get things moving. Begging your pardon, but if there's one thing I can't bear it's something falling to pieces with neglect.

BERYL. It's been such a long time.

HOOLIGAN. I suppose there's been nothing doing there for about ten years.

BERYL. I suppose it must be fifteen.

HOOLIGAN. Sure we'll get it going great guns in no time. It's just a question of clearing the undergrowth and putting in a few piledrivers.

BERYL (*overcome*). Would you like to stroll in the garden, dearest. I shall be down in just a moment.

HOOLIGAN. I might as well have a ramble and think up a few possibilities.

HOOLIGAN goes off. BERYL *moves dazedly to the door as* NED *enters.*

BERYL (*breathless*). Oh, Edward.

She goes on out. SANDRA *follows* NED *in.*

NED. What's the matter with her?

SANDRA. Heartburn.

NED. She's white as a sheet.

SANDRA. Comes over her sudden.

NED. Maybe you better go back.

SANDRA. Maybe I better stay here.

NED. Why?

SANDRA. Maybe I might never see you again.

NED. So it's not the money.

SANDRA. O.K. Hasn't been touched. (*She hands* NED *his share.*) That's your lot.

NED. Thanks.

SANDRA. Aren't you going to count it?

NED. Wait.

SANDRA. What?

NED. I can feel something.

SANDRA. What d'you mean?

NED. A whiff. The hot breath of impending doom.

SANDRA. What you on about?

NED. Last time I got it, four policemen suddenly stepped out of a wardrobe.

SANDRA. You're not up to it.

NED. C'mon, let's get rid of it.

SANDRA. Do we have to? I thought I could keep it as a souvenir.

NED. Yeh, why not put it on exhibition and sell tickets? Right. Lift. Move.

They carry it over to the window. They pull curtains aside to reveal SEDLEY.

SEDLEY. Evening, son.

NED. Hallo, Mr S. I thought you were at the Girl Guide display.

SEDLEY. Postponed.

NED. Inclement weather?

SEDLEY. No. Sixteen Brownies down with measles. The fate of many a suburban spectacular.

SANDRA. I better go. G'night, Ed.

SEDLEY *bars her way*

SEDLEY. No need to rush away, my dear. How very nice to meet you after all these weeks. I don't believe I've yet had the pleasure . . .

NED. Michelle. I'd like you to meet Mr Sedley.

SEDLEY. Hayward, actually. Edgar Hayward.

NED. Mr Hayward. This is Michelle.

SEDLEY. What a pretty name. To suit a pretty face, no doubt. Are you of Continental extraction?

SANDRA. Eh?

NED. She's a bit slow up here. Backward like.

SEDLEY. Well, not to worry, son. Youth, beauty and dumb as they come. In a bint that's not far short of perfection, to my mind. I hope I'm not interrupting anything.

NED. We were just having a bit of a clearup.

SEDLEY. So I notice. Interesting piece of equipment you've got there.

NED. Yes, I found it on a rubbish dump.

SEDLEY. Some sort of safe, isn't it?

NED. We keep our little nest egg in it.

SEDLEY. Been putting by out of your wages, eh?

NED. A bit here, a bit there. It all adds up.

SEDLEY. Yes, to a damn sight less than you just stuffed in that wallet.

NED. We just had a lucky break.

SANDRA. Dead lucky.

SEDLEY. Your pools came up.

NED. No, premium bond.

SEDLEY. Which week?

NED. Last week.

SEDLEY. Last week's winner lives in Grimsby.

NED. Was it the week before, Michelle?

SEDLEY. West Hartlepool.

NED. I beg to differ.

SEDLEY. I happen to know. I've kept one for years. There. In my wallet. Two small hostages to fortune. One premium bond. One contraceptive. God knows why. The chances of either coming up are about two million to one. (*He puts away his wallet.*) Well, well, I employ you as a decorator and you proceed to use my home as a base for criminal operations.

NED. Is that an accusation?

SEDLEY. Come off it, son, I've suspected you for weeks. (*He examines the safe.*) Convent job, eh? Not that it bothers me. Money would never have got past Rome airport anyway. How much did you get?

NED. Thirty-five quid.

SEDLEY. What about the rest of it?

NED. That goes to Mr Big.

SEDLEY. Mr Big?

NED. The mastermind of the operation. I'm just a rank and filer. I've got overheads.

SEDLEY. They're my overheads. I pay the rates.

NED. Maybe we could come to an agreement.

SEDLEY. To pervert the course of Justice? It'd be dereliction of my duty as a ratepayer.

NED. How about a fat percentage?

SEDLEY. What, of thirty-five quid? I could think of more adequate recompense for my silence than that, son.

NED. Fifty per cent.

SEDLEY. A damn sight more adequate recompense.

NED. Seventy-five.

SEDLEY. Something more in the nature of a *quid pro quo,* so to speak.

SANDRA *gets up suddenly.*

SANDRA. I better go. G'night, Ed.

SEDLEY. I'd advise her to stay.

NED. Better hang on.

SEDLEY. I thought she was slow on the uptake.

NED. She gets sudden flashes of insight.

SEDLEY. Well?

NED. What?

SEDLEY. Half an hour.

NED. What d'you mean?

SEDLEY. You know damn well what I mean. Half an hour with your lovely Michelle.

NED. On what basis?

SEDLEY. *Carte blanche.*

NED. I thought you were a photographer.

SEDLEY. I'm giving it up. I want to come to grips with reality.

NED. When?

SEDLEY. Now.

NED. How about tomorrow?

SEDLEY. She might get held up.

NED. No, it's not on.

SEDLEY. Then I shall ring the police.

NED. You don't know what you're asking.

SEDLEY. I'm not asking.

NED. She's half your age. She could be your own daughter.

SEDLEY. Yes, fascinating, isn't it?

NED. I couldn't allow it.

SEDLEY. Don't be a fool, son. She's a bint.

NED. She's my fiancée. We're engaged.

SEDLEY. Then she won't want to see you get nicked.

NED. She's a good girl. Innocent. Untouched.

SEDLEY. The state of my flowerbed indicates the contrary.

NED. I've been educating her. They're just demonstration models.

SEDLEY. She's about due for a test run then. Nothing like a premarital romp for warming the sheets.

NED. She wouldn't have it. It'll be rape.

SEDLEY. I accept that challenge.

NED. You've got a wife of your own.

SEDLEY. I know. That's the problem, son. Not the solution.

SANDRA. Oh, Ed.

NED. Let me appeal to your better instincts.

SEDLEY. I'm a deprived departmental wage slave, son. I don't have better instincts. You youngsters. Disporting like playful rabbits. The nearest I get to it is a quick trembling shufti through my Sunday newspaper. I've fallen off every escalator in London gazing at underwear advertisements. Blind fate has put you in my power, son, and I intend to make the best of it.

NED. O.K. I can arrange it. Give me ten minutes.

SEDLEY. What for?

NED. I'll put her in the picture. Spell out the odds.

SEDLEY. Good. I'll take charge of this in the meantime. (*He takes* NED's *wallet.*)

NED. You can trust me.

SEDLEY. As a sort of *bona fide*, so to speak.

NED. Ten minutes.

SEDLEY. *Carte blanche.*

NED. I'll fix it.

SEDLEY. Good. Perhaps the young lady might like to slip into something more comfortable in the interim.

NED. Comfortable?

SEDLEY. There's some black lace underwear laid out in my study.

NED. Black lace underwear?

SEDLEY. I've got something of a penchant for it.

NED. I thought you were trying to come to grips with reality.

SEDLEY. It's a start.

NED. It's a fantasy.

SEDLEY. No, an ideal, son. I'm after the unattainable.

NED. Why attain the unattainable?

SEDLEY. Because then it's attained.

NED. Then it's not unattainable.

SEDLEY. Yes, well it's not a time to argue philosophy is it, son.

You've got ten minutes. At the expiry of that period I may have
to take steps to inform the relevant authority.

SEDLEY *goes out into the hall.*

SANDRA. Thanks, Ed. You handled it beautiful.

NED. Right. Get dressed.

SANDRA. What for?

NED. Prepare to meet your maker in informal regalia.

SANDRA. What you planning?

NED. I don't know yet. I'll think of something.

SANDRA. No, I don't trust you.

NED. What you mean?

SANDRA. You might let him get me and make off with the money.

NED. Who do you think I am, Frankenstein?

SANDRA. I don't know.

NED. Well you ought to know. We've been living together for
three weeks. A relationship begins with trust.

SANDRA. We don't have a relationship.

NED. Well, let's begin with trust then.

SANDRA. Why?

NED. Maybe we'll end up with a relationship.

SANDRA. I don't want a relationship.

NED. Yes but you'd like to be able to trust me. Right leave it to
chance. I'll toss a coin. Heads you trust me. Tails you don't.
(*Tosses.*) Tails you don't.

SANDRA. Course I do.

NED. From now on.

SANDRA. How do I know you're not cheating?

NED. It's like the United Nations. Where you going?

SANDRA. I've got a headache. I'm going to bed.

NED. What about me?

SANDRA. You'll think of something.

SANDRA *goes out as* NED *dives into the study for the underwear.*

NED. What a bird, eh? At the edge of a precipice, the jaws of the
trap are closing in so what do you do?

BERYL *enters.*

Go to bed and plead a headache.

BERYL. She'll come back to you, dear. There's some blessed spirit abroad this evening that makes the impossible come true.

NED. That's what I'm afraid of.

BERYL. Benedict has declared himself.

NED. Benedict?

BERYL. Father Hooligan, dear. He wants me.

NED. What for?

BERYL. I suppose it must be for my body.

NED. What body? What you mean? For the mortuary?

BERYL. Mortuary? (HOOLIGAN *enters.*) Our go-between.

HOOLIGAN. You've paved the way, Edward.

BERYL. Thank you, dear, for bringing us together.

NED. Maybe I ought to see it through to the finish.

BERYL. Leave us, dear. We've got our own Rubicon to cross.

NED *goes out.*

HOOLIGAN. I'm happy to see there are no second thoughts.

BERYL. Suddenly I seem to have come alive.

HOOLIGAN. Strike while the iron is hot, as they say.

BERYL. I'm sure I shall repent in morning's light, but it seems so right somehow.

They sit on the sofa.

HOOLIGAN. Well, let's begin at the beginning. (*He puts on his glasses.*)

BERYL. Shall we turn out the lights?

HOOLIGAN. Sure then we couldn't see what we were up to.

BERYL. You're so forthright.

HOOLIGAN. A plain man.

BERYL. Not to me, dearest.

HOOLIGAN. Well, let's get down to business. (*He takes out some papers.*)

BERYL. What is it, dearest?

HOOLIGAN. Just a rough outline.

BERYL. Let's just let it happen, shall we?

HOOLIGAN. We might as well stick to some sort of procedure. Well now, to begin . . .

BERYL. Oh, my own.

HOOLIGAN. What's that, have you lost something?

BERYL. Only my heart, my reason.

HOOLIGAN (*intent*). Sure say a prayer to Saint Anthony and they'll turn up again in the morning.

BERYL. Let it always be night.

HOOLIGAN. What was that?

BERYL. Take me, Benedict.

HOOLIGAN. Where?

BERYL. Everywhere.

HOOLIGAN. Easy on there, now.

BERYL. My conquistador.

HOOLIGAN. I think you've had a few too many.

BERYL. No one but you.

HOOLIGAN. Pull yourself together, now. I'm a man of the cloth.

BERYL. A force of nature.

HOOLIGAN. Put it out of your head.

BERYL. It's in my heart.

HOOLIGAN. Think of your husband now.

BERYL. Never.

HOOLIGAN. You're another man's wife.

BERYL *kisses him.*

HOOLIGAN. Whatever about marriage it'd be a thousand years before we'd get the green light on this kind of thing.

BERYL. Hold me.

HOOLIGAN. Mrs Sedley. Let's get back to the matter in hand.

BERYL. Just hold my hand. A woman needs a little affection.

HOOLIGAN. I suppose there's no harm in it. (*He takes her hand.*) It'll have to stop there now.

BERYL. What bliss.

MICK *enters,* NED *drags him back.*

HOOLIGAN. What was that?

BERYL. Eternity coming to a stop.

HOOLIGAN. It sounded more like the door handle.

BERYL. Perfect peace.

HOOLIGAN. I think we're a bit exposed here. This situation is open to terrible misinterpretations.

BERYL. Come with me, dearest. I know where we can be alone.

He follows her into the study. MICK *re-enters followed by* NED.

MICK. Right, which is it, mate? In or out?

NED. In.

MICK. I don't know whether I'm coming or going.

NED. Sorry about that.

MICK. Now I'm gone again. (*He starts wandering around in a circle.*) Where am I?

NED. Eh?

MIMICK. What am I doing? Going out or coming in?

NED. Coming in.

MICK. Which way's that? I've forgotten.

NED. It's difficult to explain when you're going around in a circle.

MICK. I know it's difficult, that's why I asked you. Quickly. I got to know where I am.

NED. Where you been?

MICK. Out.

NED. Then you're coming in.

MICK. What am I facing this direction for then?

NED. Turn.

MICK. Which way?

NED. This way.

MICK. Right, I'm in. What is it?

NED. Put these on.

MICK. It's a bit late in the day for dressing up. I'm just putting Teddy to bed.

NED. Here.

He hands him the underwear.

MICK. Wait. These are meant for some kind of woman.

NED. Yeh, I know.

MICK. What are you giving them to me for?

NED. Never mind. Put 'em on.

MICK. How?

NED. Take off your clothes.

MICK. What do you mean?

NED. Strip off.

MICK. Now? In front of you?

NED. Hurry up.

MICK. Strip off in front of you and put on some clothes belonging to a woman? (*He comes up close.*) Have a cold shower, mate.

He drops them on the floor.

NED. No, wait.

MICK. Forget it. I don't want to know about it. I got my own troubles.

SANDRA *enters.*

God, you're going off, mate. Going off quick. Cuh! C'mon, Ted. Let's get ourselves out of this barrel of filth.

MICK *goes off.*

NED. What you doing here?

SANDRA. Wondered how you were getting on.

NED. You can see how I'm getting on.

SANDRA. I'll help you if you like.

NED. Why?

SANDRA. I don't know. Maybe I trust you. Maybe I don't want to see you go to prison.

NED. No? Why not?

SANDRA. I don't know.

NED. No?

SANDRA. What's happening?

NED. We're in the grip of something.

SANDRA. I don't want it to happen.

NED. I agree. It's not a time for declarations. We're up the creek.

He kisses her.

SANDRA. What did you do that for?

NED. I don't know.

SANDRA. You're the first person I've ever allowed to do that to me.

NED. You're the first person I ever wanted to do it with.

SANDRA. I didn't want to get involved.

NED. With me it was more of a question of getting there. Once I was there, a cigarette was as much as I could manage.

SANDRA. We've been doing everything backwards.

NED. Maybe we should go back to the beginning.

SANDRA. Hold hands or something.

NED. No, let's keep it for later when we get out of this bit.

SANDRA. I'll help you.

NED. No, it's too risky.

SANDRA. You wanted me to five minutes ago.

NED. I've changed.

SANDRA. You're so sudden.

NED. Lend me your hair. I'll handle it.

SANDRA *takes off her hair.* NED *puts it on.*

SANDRA. It suits you.

NED *holds up the slip.*

NED. Wait till I get into this. I'm irresistible.

SANDRA. What you planning?

NED. I don't know yet.

SANDRA *turns away as* SEDLEY *with brilliantined hair enters behind. He pauses.*

SEDLEY. Hello, my chick. What are you doing down here at this hour?

SANDRA. I had a nightmare, Dad.

SEDLEY. A nightmare?

SANDRA. I dreamt a wicked man was trying to get me into his room.

SEDLEY. Nonsense. Wherever do you get such ideas? Things like that don't happen in our little nest. Run along now.

SANDRA. G'night, Dad.

Exit SANDRA

SEDLEY. Well?
NED. O.K.
SEDLEY. Is she in there?
NED. All fixed up.
SEDLEY. You mentioned about the . . .
NED. All togged out.
SEDLEY. Good.
NED. I've kept my side of the bargain.
SEDLEY. Very well then.

He is about to hand NED *the money when the study door opens and* HOOLIGAN *emerges.*

HOOLIGAN. Edward.
NED. Yes, Chief?
HOOLIGAN. I'm afraid our benefactress lies prostrate.
NED. O.K., Chief.
HOOLIGAN (*to* SEDLEY). Goodnight to you sir.

He goes on out.

NED. She's ready for you now.
SEDLEY. Who was that?
NED. That's Mr Big.
SEDLEY. What's he doing there?
NED. Just checking out.
SEDLEY. What?
NED. The rules.
SEDLEY. What rules?
NED. I'll have that.

He takes the money.

SEDLEY. What rules?

NED *opens the door.*

NED. No talking.

SEDLEY. Eh?

NED. No lights. (*He shepherds him in.*) You've got twenty minutes. Make the most of it.

He clicks off the light switch.

Blackout

CURTAIN

ACT THREE

The following morning. Ladders stacked against wall.
NED *listening intently at* SEDLEY's *door, turns away and starts to put on his shirt as* MICK's *head comes around windows.*

MICK. Here.

NED. What?

MICK. It's today, en' it?

NED. Today?

MICK. I mean, it's not yesterday.

NED. No.

MICK. How about tomorrow?

NED. Hasn't arrived yet.

MICK. That's what I thought. (*Enters.*) Spot on again, eh? I reckon that's the secret of living, mate. Knowing where you are.

NED. Yeh?

MICK. Trouble is, I get to that point, I start getting worried sick again.

NED. Why's that?

MICK. Well, what do I do next?

NED. How about clearing that stuff away?

MICK. Thanks, mate. Thought I was stuck in another log jam there. Finishing up then?

NED. Yeh, I'm leaving.

MICK. Leaving? Not a chance, mate. They got dogs out there, barbed wire. Searchlights. You'll be torn to pieces before getting burned to a crisp.

NED. I'll risk it.

MICK. It's all right for you, chum. I got the job of sweeping you up afterwards. I'm busy enough as it is without worrying about mop, bucket, hosepipe, dustpan . . .

NED. Go on, clear out of it.

MICK. 'Strewth. Day's hardly begun and I'm up to me eyes.

Enter SANDRA *in school uniform, smoking.*

SANDRA. Morning.

MICK. Yeh, I know, doll. I'm not that stupid. I see the light.

Exit MICK *with a ladder.*

SANDRA. How's it going?

NED. You've got a baby brother coming along.

SANDRA. He'll have problems. What happened, then?

NED. Don't know. He's not up yet.

SANDRA. Must be sleeping it off.

NED. Or planning a sweet revenge.

SANDRA. Me Mum's upstairs.

NED. How does she look?

SANDRA. Same as ever.

NED. Fulfilled? Unfulfilled? What's she doing?

SANDRA. Gargling.

NED. That's a big help.

SANDRA. Anyway, it doesn't show on your face, does it? Otherwise I'd have been thrown out years ago. When you off?

NED. Soon as I get my papers.

SANDRA. Oh, about last night. We got a bit carried away.

NED. Yeh?

SANDRA. What I mean is, I've got my own plans. I'm afraid you're not included.

NED. I'll get over it.

SANDRA. You're a bit boring for me.

NED. It's the life I lead. Sitting and waiting.

SANDRA. Ought to be used to it by now.

NED. Yeh, I get this on every job, don't I? Five hundred quid invested in a parental rave-up.

SANDRA. It's your idea.

NED. What I get myself into, eh? My whole future depending on something like this. It's like waiting for the results of your own conception.

Enter BERYL *in a summer dress.*

BERYL. My, what a beautiful day, children! I believe there's a hint of Spring in the air.

SANDRA. Mum what you done to yourself? You look great.

BERYL. Do I, dear?

NED. Ten years younger.

Enter MICK.

BERYL. Thank you, Edward.

SANDRA. Like a film star.

NED. Fantastic.

MICK. Tart.

SANDRA. How did you manage it, Mum?

BERYL. Someday, when you're a woman, dear, maybe I'll tell you.

SANDRA. I can't wait.

BERYL. Run along, dear.

Exit SANDRA.

Poor lamb. If she knew at what cost my beauty had been achieved. Oh, Edward, I'm that confused I don't know which way to turn.

MICK. I got that problem. What you got to do is stop, turn right round, figure out where you just been and forget it. There's no way out of this dump either way.

Exit MICK *with a second ladder.*

BERYL. I expect you've guessed what came to pass.

NED. I'm putting it together.

BERYL. What madness! I thought he'd left and next minute . . .

NED. I'm pleased and happy for you, Mrs S.

BERYL. Where it shall all end I can't imagine. Did Mr Sedley arrive home safely?

NED. Shortly after midnight.

BERYL. He must never know what happened, Edward.

NED. Yeh, I go along with that.

BERYL. Thank you, dear. To think it should come to this. Deceiving my own husband. And yet I'm not a deceitful person.

It's as if it's all part of some dream, some impossible dream from which one need never awaken.

Enter SEDLEY, *neatly dressed, with a buttonhole.*

SEDLEY. Good morning, my dear.

BERYL, Why, George. What a surprise! I thought you'd have left for the department.

SEDLEY. A slight indisposition, my love.

NED. I believe there's a lot of it about this weather.

SEDLEY. I dare say we might allow temporary right of way from time to time. What an attractive dress you're wearing, Beryl!

BERYL. Why thank you, George. It does suit you, that buttonhole.

NED. Nothing like a touch of it for getting the juices going.

SEDLEY. I beg your pardon, son.

NED. Spring.

BERYL. Well, I really must be getting on. Goodbye, George.

SEDLEY. Goodbye, my dear.

Exit BERYL.

What's the matter with her, then?

NED. I think she's knocked out by your new image.

SEDLEY. Looks like she's seen a ghost.

NED. Must be something of an occasion, eh?

SEDLEY. Eh? Well, decency forbids, son. After all the lady is your fiancée. Still I don't mind saying if I'd married someone like that my whole life might have proved different.

NED. Yeh?

SEDLEY. I could have faced each day with confidence and zest. What age did you say she was again?

NED. Sixteen.

SEDLEY. Funny, she seemed a bit . . . how can I put it?

NED. What?

SEDLEY. Ample? A bit more there than I'd imagined.

NED. Optical illusion on account of the dark.

SEDLEY. She left this.

He produces a large black corset.

NED. Thanks.

SEDLEY. A bit roomy, wouldn't you say?

NED. Roomy?

SEDLEY. You'd fit three of her inside of this, son.

NED. Maybe you got rolled up in it too without knowing.

SEDLEY. Yes, I dare say. It was that sort of evening.

NED. Rough, eh?

SEDLEY. Well, we'd best draw a veil over what happened in there last night, son. It's enough to say I walked in the door and thought I'd run into a mechanical excavator.

NED. Command performance, eh?

SEDLEY. Not to mention the encore. My word, you young people. No wonder you're all incapable of putting in a decent day's work. I've had to apply for two days leave.

NED. I'd say that entitled me to a refund.

SEDLEY. No chance of you staying on for a bit, I suppose?

NED. What for?

SEDLEY. Maybe you'd care to do the whole house.

NED. Who needs renovating, you or the house?

SEDLEY. The fact is I'm a bit loth to see you go just now.

NED. I can imagine.

SEDLEY. You don't take out a new car and do a ton down the motorway straight off. I could do with a couple of weeks cruising at thirty miles an hour.

NED. Be happy to oblige but I'm afraid she's left.

SEDLEY. Left?

NED. Got an au pair job in Huddersfield.

SEDLEY. Well, that is a blow.

NED. I'll get over it.

SEDLEY. You've let quite a treasure slip through your fingers there, son. No chance of a reconciliation? A few flowers, perhaps?

NED. Not a chance.

SEDLEY. Well, that's that then.

NED. Afraid so.

SEDLEY. Never rains but it pours, does it. Now I'm faced with another long period of drought.

NED. Oh, I don't know.

SEDLEY. Not going to find something like that in a hurry.

NED. Something may turn up.

SEDLEY. Not a chance. There's many a night I've gone down on my knees and prayed for something like that to come striding, God knows why, up my front path. I might as well have dialled directory enquiries and requested an archangel.

Enter HOOLIGAN

HOOLIGAN. Isn't that a wonderful morning, Mr Sedley. It does you good to climb through a tree with the sun on your back.

SEDLEY. I'd be obliged if you'd inform this gentleman this is a private residence, son. Not some sort of underworld rendezvous.

Exit SEDLEY.

NED. He's a bit of a tartar.

HOOLIGAN. He seems generous enough. That's a great pile of money you have there.

NED. Been putting in some overtime.

HOOLIGAN. The labourer is worthy of his hire, as they say. I have your release papers in my pocket.

NED. That's pleasant news, Padre.

HOOLIGAN. Sure, it's happy days all round, Edward. The garden is in the bag. We've done the Vicar in the eye and no mistake. The Mother Superior is beside herself. Extra helpings of porridge for the novices and bacon and eggs for myself. It was as good as a canonization. Is the lady of the house about?

NED. I'm afraid she's not up yet.

HOOLIGAN. We'd best be on our way. I've to catch the boat train. To tell you the truth, I've had enough of feminine wiles for a bit. I'm afraid we've been dealing with something of a *femme fatale*, as they say.

Enter BERYL.

Speak of the angels, Mrs Sedley.

BERYL. Oh, it's you, Father.

HOOLIGAN. You'd better collect your things.

Exit NED.

I thought I'd better pay my final respects.

BERYL. Oh, are you going away somewhere?

HOOLIGAN. I'm on my way back to Africa. Mission accomplished, so to speak.

BERYL. That is a blow, I suppose.

HOOLIGAN. I'll be passing you on to my successor. Father Mooney from Hong Kong.

BERYL. Truth has come with the dawn, hasn't it? Still I expect it's for the best really. I've not been without pangs of conscience.

HOOLIGAN. Is there something bothering you?

BERYL. I expect it'll pass when I get to confession.

HOOLIGAN. That'll be tricky. Mooney won't get in till the end of the month. Your best bet is the Holy Friars. They run a round-the-clock emergency service.

BERYL. I'd best go there this evening.

HOOLIGAN. It's a bit of a journey. Are you in a very bad way then?

BERYL. It is something of a burden.

HOOLIGAN. Sure I've a few minutes to spare. I'll tell you what, Mrs Sedley. I'll confess you myself.

BERYL. It is good of you to offer, Father. But I could quite easily go to the monastery.

HOOLIGAN. One good turn deserves another as they say.

BERYL. Yes, but can it be valid, Father? Under the circumstances?

HOOLIGAN. I suppose it's a bit irregular. But after ten years in Africa you don't worry about the proprieties. I've confessed many a sinner in the prow of a canoe. Kneel down there and we'll fix up something.

BERYL. Well, if you're quite sure, Father.

BERYL *kneels.* HOOLIGAN *adopts confessional pose.*

HOOLIGAN. Now you must try and think of me merely as an intermediary. And remember every word you say I'll have forgotten the minute you've said it. Go ahead now.

BERYL. Bless me it is one week since my last confession.

HOOLIGAN. Good, good.

BERYL. Well, I've told a fib or two and indulged in vain thoughts and . . . oh dear, this is the difficult bit.

HOOLIGAN. We hear all kinds of things this side of the grille.

BERYL. I've been unfaithful to my marriage vow.

HOOLIGAN. In what way?

BERYL. I've broken the Sixth Commandment.

HOOLIGAN. You probably only gave it a bit of a dent.

BERYL. I've parted with my virtue, I'm afraid.

HOOLIGAN. When was this?

BERYL. Last night.

HOOLIGAN. You're not referring to a bit of handholding by any chance?

BERYL. No, it was later than that.

HOOLIGAN. And what happened exactly?

BERYL. Everything.

HOOLIGAN. Everything?

BERYL. Twice.

HOOLIGAN. I beg your pardon?

BERYL. Everything that can happen.

HOOLIGAN. And who was the other party concerned? Was he a married man?

BERYL. No, Father. I'm afraid he was a man of God.

HOOLIGAN. What do you mean, some kind of clergyman?

BERYL. Yes, Father.

HOOLIGAN. Are you sure you're not making the whole thing up?

BERYL. Quite sure, Father. A woman takes note of such things.

HOOLIGAN. This is a devilish business. I suspect that this gentleman isn't so much after your body as something else entirely.

BERYL. Really, Father?

HOOLIGAN. I'm afraid there are ulterior motives at work. So you must build yourself into a tower of strength to resist his advances. And whatever he proposes, don't sign your name. Are you in the habit of reading romantic literature?

BERYL. I do keep a favourite novel at my bedside.

HOOLIGAN. You'd best put it aside and try a chapter of the Old Testament. It's got as much passion, rape and high romance as all the others put together. That'll put you on the right road. Very well now, you're absolved.

BERYL *rises*.

BERYL. It is such a relief, isn't it?

HOOLIGAN. It'll tide you over for a few days anyway. Now, about our own little affair, have you told your husband yet?

BERYL. Are you still speaking as my confessor?

HOOLIGAN. Indeed no. As a grateful friend to a benefactress.

BERYL. I'm afraid I haven't been quite able to bring myself.

HOOLIGAN. You'd better let him know as soon as possible. It'll avoid complications for Mooney later on. Would you like a little moral support?

Enter NED.

BERYL. I'd best tell him myself, if you don't mind, Father.

Exit BERYL.

NED. All set.

HOOLIGAN. There's been a bit of a hitch, Edward. I suspect the Vicar is resorting to desperate methods. I'll let her break the news to Mr Sedley and then present him with a *fait accompli*, so to speak.

NED. I'd advise against it. He's a tricky customer.

HOOLIGAN. Sure I'm a skilled negotiator, Edward.

NED. Leave it to me. I'll soften him up. You got my papers?

HOOLIGAN *hands over the papers*.

HOOLIGAN. Don't be too long about it.

Enter SANDRA *in school uniform*.

NED. Give me five minutes.

Exit HOOLIGAN.

Right, I'm off.

SANDRA. Got everything?

NED. One step ahead of the avalanche.

SANDRA *puts on her wig and glasses.*

SANDRA. Well, g'bye.

NED. See you.

SANDRA. Afraid I got nothing to say really.

NED. Me neither.

SANDRA. We never got through to each other.

NED. Nothing much there to get through to.

SANDRA. You're a bit old.

NED. You're underdeveloped.

SANDRA. Be past it in a couple of years.

NED. I ought to be taking on birds with standard equipment.

SANDRA. Well . . .

NED. That's it then.

SANDRA. Bit of a letdown, really.

NED. Yeh.

SANDRA. Expect it's my fault. I don't need anyone really.

NED. I'm a bit of a loner myself.

SANDRA. Thought you were going.

NED. So did I.

SANDRA. Oh no, not again.

NED. I'm afraid we're stuck with some blind, primitive instinct.

SANDRA. But I don't want to get involved.

NED. What about me? I've got plans.

SANDRA. I'm not going off with you.

NED. That's all I need, en' it. Stuck with a school kid.

SANDRA. What would we live on?

NED. Right back to the small time.

SANDRA. Flogging pot from a windowbox.

NED. Pitiful. You'd need a garden at least.

SANDRA. Yeh, but that'd mean living in the suburbs.

NED. Getting a mortgage.

SANDRA. We might have to get married.

NED. Yeh. Qualify for the Benefit.

SANDRA. Have kids.

NED. Grab hold of the family allowance.

SANDRA. We'd have to train them to bring stuff home from Woolworths.

NED. And there may not always be a Woolworths.

SANDRA. Be even worse later on.

NED. Yeh. Can't retire if you haven't been working.

SEDLEY *enters through the windows. Halts.*

SANDRA. We'd have to grow old together.

NED. Die. Qualify for the burial grant.

SANDRA. Well . . .

NED. That's it.

SANDRA. Yeh.

NED. Hurry up.

SANDRA. I'll get my things.

SANDRA *takes off her wig and glasses as* SEDLEY *enters, takes up wig and leaves it down in disbelief.*

SEDLEY. Say it isn't true, son.

NED. Cigarette?

SEDLEY. What freak of nature have you perpetrated?

NED. I'm afraid there's been a little lighthearted deception.

SEDLEY. Lighthearted? What am I to believe, son. That I've corrupted my own daughter?

NED. Nothing like that.

SANDRA. What d'you mean, Dad?

SEDLEY. Right. Let's have it, son, before I tear you apart. Who?

NED. A last-minute substitute.

SEDLEY. Substitute?

NED. Well I couldn't very well provide the original, could I. Name of Marlene. I put her in at short notice.

SEDLEY. Leave the room, child, I'll deal with this ruffian.

Exit SANDRA.

How can I believe you?

NED. You may recall she's a bit on the hefty side. She's a trainee policewoman.

SEDLEY. 'Strewth, you've got some explaining to do and no mistake. What, you stand here last night and let me proposition my own daughter?

NED. I didn't exactly encourage it, did I?

SEDLEY. What was she doing down here last night?

NED. Helping me clear up.

SEDLEY. You introduced her as somebody else.

NED. You introduced yourself as somebody else.

SEDLEY. How long has she been dressing up like that, then?

NED. I don't know, Mr S. I'm only the decorator, en' I?

SEDLEY. You've had her, son. You've had my daughter.

NED. Her? She's only a kid.

SEDLEY. You've been knocking around with her for weeks.

NED. We've had the odd bit of chat. I've been a sort of elder brother to her.

SEDLEY. Do you expect me to believe that? With your appetites?

NED. You've got a vivid imagination.

SEDLEY. With the souvenirs you leave laying about I don't need an imagination. What are you, son, eh? To pluck a delicate blossom and cast it aside without a backward glance?

NED. I think you're watching the wrong kind of programmes.

SEDLEY. I ought to tear you limb from limb. But I've got a better idea.

NED. What you on about?

SEDLEY. I'm turning you in.

NED. We've got an agreement.

SEDLEY. I'm revoking it.

NED. I think you're forgetting something.

SEDLEY. What?

NED. You've fulfilled your share of the contract.

SEDLEY. What, some faceless policewoman? What's that got to do with my daughter?

NED. She's somebody's daughter too.

SEDLEY. Somebody else's daughter. Not my problem.

NED. I take it you disapprove of the Common Market then?

SEDLEY. You'll not deflect me with irrelevancy, son.

NED. I could inform somebody's wife.

SEDLEY. You keep my wife out of this. You've brought enough trouble to this household. I'm making a phone call, son.

NED. I'll get Marlene to bring an allegation then.

SEDLEY. I dare say it'll be believed. With your background.

NED. I've got another witness. Mr Big.

SEDLEY. What, a criminal? I'm married to a householder. That means something in this part of the world.

NED. He's a man of consequence.

SEDLEY. What are you attempting to do, threaten me?

NED. We could keep this up all day, Mr S. Fact is, I'm in a hurry. I've got to leave.

SEDLEY. You're not leaving, son. It'd be a mockery of parenthood to let you out of here unscathed. Messing with my daughter.

NED. I assure you you're mistaken.

SEDLEY. I can't take the risk. You know my views on the subject.

NED. This is where you wheel in the appliance.

SEDLEY. I don't need an appliance. (*He takes a revolver from a drawer.*) I've got this.

NED. What's that for.

SEDLEY. Over against the wall, son. You've got a fair share of explaining to do. Now, let's have the truth.

Enter BERYL *with a sherry tray.*

What is it, Beryl?

BERYL. I thought you might care for a glass of sherry, dear.

SEDLEY. It's hardly appropriate. I suspect this young thug of having designs on our daughter.

BERYL. If that were all that was amiss, George.

SEDLEY. Am I to understand you condone his behaviour?

BERYL. I'm afraid it's but the tip of the iceberg, dear.

SEDLEY. What iceberg?

Enter HOOLIGAN.

F

HOOLIGAN. The Lord's blessing on the family assembled.

BERYL. Put away your gun, George. We've got the neighbours to consider.

HOOLIGAN. I thought you might need a helping hand.

SEDLEY. Are you acquainted with this person, Beryl?

BERYL. I'm afraid so, George.

SEDLEY. I fail to see what business you have with this denizen of the underworld.

HOOLIGAN. That's one way of putting it, I suppose.

SEDLEY. I believe I'm addressing the mastermind behind the convent job.

HOOLIGAN. That's correct.

BERYL. I expect I'd better introduce you.

SEDLEY. Your protegé here has already done the honours. Mr Big, I believe.

HOOLIGAN. Big?

NED. A sort of tactful alias, chief, bearing in mind . . . (*Indicates collar.*)

HOOLIGAN. I suppose it's time to reveal my true colours, Mrs Sedley.

BERYL. This is Father Hooligan, dear.

SEDLEY. Eh?

BERYL. Father Hooligan from the convent.

SEDLEY. Well that doesn't surprise me.

BERYL. I hope his profession will not be cause for offence.

SEDLEY. On the contrary. It's an unexpected pleasure to meet the proof of your prejudices face to face.

HOOLIGAN. I'm pleased to meet you, Mr Sedley.

NED. Perhaps I could suggest a glass of sherry?

BERYL. Yes, Edward. After all we're civilized people, aren't we? We can discuss these things.

SEDLEY. Well, I thought your predecessor was a card but you take the perpetual candle, eh, Reverend? Robbing your own poorbox, leading a bunch of teenage ruffians. That's spreading the ecumenical spirit a bit thick.

HOOLIGAN. Sure a spot of anti-clericalism never did anyone any harm.

SEDLEY. Well, you're looking healthy enough on it, I must say.

NED *dispenses drinks*.

HOOLIGAN. Well, Edward. I gather we're running into a little opposition.

NED. Shaping up that way, Boss.

BERYL. Well, it is pleasant to be able to get together, isn't it?

HOOLIGAN. Well, Mr Sedley, to proceed to the heart of the matter.

SEDLEY. Yes, I'm assuming you're not here for refreshment.

HOOLIGAN. Your good lady and I have been putting our heads together.

BERYL. Forgive me, George.

HOOLIGAN. As you know, the Holy Sisters are anxious to extend their funerary arrangements.

SEDLEY. Yes, I've no doubt. It's like a battlefield out there. Elbows sticking up all over the place.

HOOLIGAN. And your wife, in her generosity, is prepared to alleviate this by bestowing her garden for that purpose.

BERYL. Our garden, Father?

HOOLIGAN. As a deed of gift. We'd naturally appreciate your consent to this arrangement.

BERYL. Oh, George.

SEDLEY. And if I refuse?

HOOLIGAN. I'm sure I've no wish to cause any marital dissent.

SEDLEY. Well, that seems clear enough. Well, you're a credit to your cloth and no mistake, Reverend. Compromising your parishioners to obtain their property for the Church. 'Strewth what a treat for the Sundays.

HOOLIGAN. That's hardly the correct interpretation.

BERYL. Is this your ulterior motive, Father?

SEDLEY. Still, I dare say it's in the best of clerical tradition. I believe the Vatican City was procured in a similar manner. Well, Beryl, I can't think what allegation this gentleman is about to bring but I think we can treat it with the contempt it deserves.

BERYL. No, George, I'm afraid it's true.

SEDLEY. True, my love?

BERYL. Oh, George, it is difficult to bring myself to say it but I'm afraid something happened last night. In your study, dear.

SEDLEY. Hardly anything to make a fuss about, my love.

BERYL. Oh, if only that were the case.

SEDLEY. A little light flirtation perhaps?

BERYL. No, George. I'm afraid I've been unfaithful.

SEDLEY. I beg your pardon, Beryl?

BERYL. Unfaithful. I've been having an affair.

SEDLEY. What sort of an affair?

BERYL. An affair of the heart. Or more truthfully an affair of the body. I've given myself to someone.

SEDLEY. What, last night? In my study?

NED. I believe you were at a gymnastic display.

SEDLEY. You seem well acquainted with my wife's movements, son. What am I to think, that you've been having her as well?

HOOLIGAN. Perhaps I've come at an inappropriate moment.

BERYL. Not Edward, dear. Flattered though I am you should think it possible. With this other gentleman.

SEDLEY. What, the Reverend?

HOOLIGAN. I'm afraid I must correct that impression. It was another clerical gentleman, I regret to say.

BERYL. Must we betray each other, Benedict?

HOOLIGAN. Sparing the confessional, but I'm not the only clergyman who was here last night.

SEDLEY. Well, this is a startling revelation, Beryl.

BERYL. I expect it must be, dear.

SEDLEY. I can't think when I've been so taken aback. Carrying on with the local clergy, what am I to make of it?

BERYL. I don't know, George. I expect I'm going through some sort of stage.

SEDLEY. Stage?

BERYL. Well, like the seven year itch, George, only perhaps the next one along.

SEDLEY. I'd hardly have thought you were capable.

BERYL. Neither would I, dear.

SEDLEY. You've not exactly shown tendencies in that direction, I must say.

BERYL. I suppose I've discovered I'm a woman.

SEDLEY. Well, it's a bit late in the game for that, Beryl. It might have been more appropriately discovered at the time of our marriage.

HOOLIGAN. I think a little Christian forgiveness might be in order.

SEDLEY. I'd be obliged if you'd stay out of this, Reverend. A fine state of affairs your Gospel has got my family into. Wife and daughter up the stick.

HOOLIGAN. I feel your view of the Faith is a little distorted, Mr Sedley.

Enter SANDRA.

SEDLEY. Yes, well I've no doubt you're too steeped in your life of crime to be capable of reform, Reverend. As for this young thug, I intend to see that he's brought to justice on the charge of corrupting my daughter.

SANDRA. Someone to see you, Dad.

SEDLEY. Who is it?

SANDRA. She says her name is Marlene.

Enter MICK *dressed in* SANDRA's *long dress, glasses, wig, etc. He advances down to confront* SEDLEY. *Chews sweets vacantly. Pirouettes. Shrugs. Turns back up. Collects more sweets from* SANDRA. *He goes off followed by* SANDRA.

BERYL. Are you acquainted with that young lady, dear?

SEDLEY. Acquainted, my love?

NED. I'm afraid we've got another revelation coming up.

BERYL. Oh, George. Have you been unfaithful too?

SEDLEY. Hardly more than a momentary encounter, my dear.

HOOLIGAN. I seem to have stumbled into a hornet's nest as they say.

BERYL. To think it should come to this. Have you often had recourse to this procedure?

SEDLEY. I never met her prior to last night, Beryl.

BERYL. Last night? What irony, George. To think we should have lapsed together.

HOOLIGAN. I suppose it's a kind of judgement, Mrs Sedley.

BERYL. Our marriage must be at a cross-roads, George.

SEDLEY. Cross roads? It went through the red light and into a layby years ago, my love.

BERYL. To think we should all seek for love elsewhere.

SEDLEY. It's not without provocation, is it, Beryl?

BERYL. I shall not reproach you, dear. I expect we've been building up to it over the years. There's not been much of that side to our marriage, when you look back.

SEDLEY. What side?

BERYL. That side. I expect it all began with our honeymoon.

SEDLEY. It all finished up with our honeymoon as I recall.

BERYL. I was but a girl. Perhaps if you'd given me more time.

SEDLEY. I'd have thought fourteen days in Clacton were ample time, my love.

BERYL. It was my upbringing. I was brought up to believe that men were only after the one thing.

SEDLEY. Well, that's hardly a matter for dispute.

BERYL. I realize that now, George. Perhaps it's all been for the best really. I expect it's things like this that bring a family together?

SEDLEY. I find that a bit hard to believe.

HOOLIGAN. Sure it's the healing hand of Providence, Mr Sedley. He works in strange ways. And what a wonderful thing it would be now to offer him something in return.

SEDLEY. I'd spare us the hand of Providence, Reverend. If you're a typical representative, it looks as if Lucifer's back in charge.

BERYL. Let us not waste time in reproaches. We've got the future to contend with. Must we live apart, George?

SEDLEY. I'm sure we've no need to take such drastic measures.

BERYL. We've got our daughter to consider. A broken home. We don't want her turning into a problem child.

SEDLEY. I'm not sure this young man hasn't started her off already.

NED. I feel she was merely seeking the affection denied her.

BERYL. I expect he's right. There's not been much love to spare within these walls. Well, George?

SEDLEY. Yes, my love?

BERYL. I expect we'll just have to go on.

HOOLIGAN. Sure it's never too late to start afresh.

BERYL. Perhaps this can be the start of a new beginning.

HOOLIGAN. Then I take it the garden is likely to remain where it is?

SEDLEY. I'd be obliged if you'd drop that hymn of praise, Reverend. I've got enough on your lot to fill a month of Sundays.

BERYL. Well, that has been a pleasant little chat. I expect it's helped to clear the air, really. (*Rises.*) Oh, dear, I feel quite overcome. Would you open a window, George?

SEDLEY *opens the windows.*

SEDLEY. Take my advice, Reverend, you'll transfer your activities to other climes.

HOOLIGAN. Indeed, I'm on my way back to Africa.

SEDLEY. Yes, your sort does very well in the colonies. Meanwhile, I'd be obliged if you and your entourage would vacate the premises.

SEDLEY *goes off.*

HOOLIGAN. I'll bid my farewells, Mrs Sedley.

BERYL. Goodbye, Father. I do hope you've enjoyed your visit to our shores.

HOOLIGAN. I suppose you could say my true heart lies in Africa.

BERYL. It wasn't to be, was it?

HOOLIGAN. Once you've got used to the call of the wild it's difficult to be satisfied with a few tame squirrels.

BERYL. Goodbye, Benedict.

She goes off.

HOOLIGAN. So, in the heel of the hunt, our efforts have come to naught. Still the garden isn't likely to shift. Half a loaf as they say.

NED. Sorry about that, Padre.

HOOLIGAN. To tell you the truth, I'll be glad to get shut of the place. You're nearer to God's heart in a jungle when all's said and done. You'd find more decency among a colony of apes. Where are you headed?

NED. Up West.

HOOLIGAN. I suppose you'll come to no harm. If you got through three weeks in this place without straying you could face Sodom and Gomorrah without batting an eye.

HOOLIGAN *goes off. Enter* SEDLEY.

SEDLEY. I thought I ordered you out of here.

NED. All right. Give me a minute.

SEDLEY. Well, I think you might have spared me that, son.

NED. Fair do's, Mr S.

SEDLEY. At least I'd have been left with the memory. I thought I'd had forbidden fruit not a barrowload of mashed potato.

NED. Best I could do at short notice.

SEDLEY. Yes, I dare say.

NED. Anyway, you don't have any problems in that direction now, do you?

SEDLEY. Eh?

NED. Sorry. None of my business, is it?

SEDLEY. What you getting at?

NED. Well, if the Padre's recommendation is anything to go by, that's quite a wife you've got there.

SEDLEY. Eh?

NED. Looks like you've been sitting half your life on a gold-mine.

SEDLEY. Yes, well I'm obliged for the information, son, but you'd best clear off out of here before I put you in charge.

NED. No offence. Well, good luck, Mr S. Thanks for everything. Been quite an experience in many ways.

SEDLEY. Yes, well I dare say you've done a reasonable job, son. But I think next time I might be better advised to call in a professional.

SEDLEY *goes off. Enter* SANDRA.

SANDRA. Right. We going?

NED. Don't have much choice, do we?

SANDRA. No.

NED. What do we try when the money runs out? Parking meters?

SANDRA. I've been doing a bit of preliminary planning.

NED. Planning?

SANDRA *produces a newspaper photo.*

SANDRA. What d'you think of that?

NED. Where is it, Buckingham Palace?

SANDRA. No.

NED. Where?

SANDRA. Bank of England.

NED. It's a thought.

SANDRA. Interested?

NED. I might be.

SANDRA. Thought you would.

NED. What about the army of computers guarding the vaults?

SANDRA. Computers? We've got better than that.

Enter MICK.

MICK. What's up?

NED. We're leaving.

MICK. Ask me to dress up, I kick your teeth right down your throat.

NED. Forget it.

MICK. Oh yeh, you're leaving, I forgot. Which way you going? Up?

NED. I can't fly.

MICK. You don't have to fly, mate. What's flying got to do with it.
Who put that stupid idea in your head? Listen. (*Confidentially*.)
Outside, against the wall, a ladder. Right? Up the ladder and
on to the roof. Across the roof to the top of the roof there's a
pipe sticking up. On top of the pipe, a bird. Thump the bird,
into the pipe and shoot out the bottom boot first, knock over
the dog and cross to the barbed wire. Don't-touch-any-metal.
Till you get to the yard. Then, up the steps, turn left, there's a
door, there's a window. Ignore the window, kick in the door
and you know where you are?

NED. Where?

MICK. Right back where you started. Right back in this bloody
room. I know. I've tried it.

NED. Thanks.

MICK. Good luck. You'll need it. (*Shaking hands*.) Think you can
make it? All the way?

NED. Sure, why not?

MICK. Oh. Well, what we shaking hands for? You'll be back here
again in five minutes.

NED. You're coming too.

MICK. No, I'm here already ... It would be a stupid waste of
time.

SANDRA. Here, I'll handle him. (*She rummages in her bag and
gives him a key*.) They said to give you this.

MICK. What you mean?

SANDRA. They're letting you out.

MICK. What, out the front way? In style?

SANDRA. You're free.

MICK. For good? No guards? No searchlights? How do I know?

SANDRA. They gave you the key.

MICK. About time, en' it? I been sorting myself out long enough.
(*To Key*.) Glad to see you, mate. You're a real friend, and why
wouldn't you be, we're in the same line of business, en't we?
Can I keep him?

SANDRA. He's yours.

MICK (*stuffs it in his pocket*). There you are, Ted. Now there's three of us.

He starts to go off with NED *and* SANDRA *as* BERYL *enters.*

BERYL. Are you going off somewhere, dear?

NED. Yeh, we've sort of decided to elope.

BERYL. Elope? Oh dear, I'm afraid it's one of those days, isn't it? Are you very much in love?

SANDRA. With him? Of course not.

NED. That's why we're eloping.

BERYL. I beg your pardon?

NED. We feel it might inject a little romance into our relationship.

BERYL. You young people. You do seem to be able to get a grip on things. Love will find a way, there's no gainsaying it. I suppose I better give you my blessing. How old are you now, dear?

SANDRA. Fifteen.

BERYL. You're far too young. Whatever will your father think?

NED. I'll look after her.

BERYL. See that she completes her O levels. He would have wanted that.

NED. I'll put her down for a comprehensive.

BERYL. Be careful crossing the road.

SANDRA. I will, Mum.

BERYL. Keep in touch.

NED. Maybe you could come up the odd weekend.

BERYL. Could I, dear? To London? What an impossible dream. I expect it has changed since the Coronation. Better hurry dear before your father comes in. Write him a hurried explanation. He's always been one for the proprieties. Goodbye, Edward.

NED. So long, Mrs S.

MICK *kisses her hand.*

MICK. I liked you. You were my kind of person.

BERYL. Are you eloping too?

MICK. Yeh, me and Ted. I reckon we could make it.

SANDRA. Cheerio, Mum.

BERYL. Goodbye, my chick. Try and be happy together. Remember I shall be living through the three of you.

NED, SANDRA *and* MICK *go off.* BERYL *waves with her handkerchief, dries her eyes.*

Oh dear, I really must be getting on.

Selects a black slip from an identical pile over her arm, slips out of her housecoat, disclosing another black slip, as SEDLEY *enters, watches speculatively, clears his throat.*

Why, you startled me, George.

SEDLEY. Just disposing of some refuse.

BERYL. Well, what's done is done and can't be undone, George.

SEDLEY. Yes, I dare say. I wasn't aware that you possessed such an array of black lace underwear, my dear.

BERYL. It's by mistake, really. I made a wrong entry in the mail order catalogue.

SEDLEY. It's a mistake that greatly becomes you, my dear.

BERYL. Thank you, George.

SEDLEY. Is our little daughter on the premises?

BERYL. I'm afraid she's just eloped with that Edward.

SEDLEY. Oh. Would you care to vacuum out my room?

BERYL. That would be a pleasure, dear. It has been quite a time, hasn't it?

SEDLEY. Quite a considerable time, my love. Allow me.

He takes up the cleaner.

BERYL. Why, thank you, George.

SEDLEY. My pleasure, Beryl.

BERYL *goes into the study.* SEDLEY *takes the key out of the door; slips it in his vest pocket, goes in and closes the door behind him.*

CURTAIN

Methuen's Modern Plays

EDITED BY JOHN CULLEN

Paul Ableman	*Green Julia*
Jean Anouilh	*Antigone*
	Becket
	Poor Bitos
	Ring Round the Moon
	The Lark
	The Rehearsal
	The Fighting Cock
John Arden	*Serjeant Musgrave's Dance*
	The Workhouse Donkey
	Armstrong's Last Goodnight
	Left-handed Liberty
	Soldier, Soldier and other plays
	Two Autobiographical Plays
John Arden and	*The Business of Good Government*
Margaretta D'Arcy	*The Royal Pardon*
	The Hero Rises Up
Ayckbourn, Bowen, Brook, Campton, Melly, Owen, Pinter, Saunders, Weldon	*Mixed Doubles*
Brendan Behan	*The Quare Fellow*
	The Hostage
Barry Bermange	*No Quarter and The Interview*
Edward Bond	*Saved*
	Narrow Road to the Deep North
	The Pope's Wedding
John Bowen	*Little Boxes*
	The Disorderly Women
Bertolt Brecht	*Mother Courage*
	The Caucasian Chalk Circle
	The Good Person of Szechwan
	The Life of Galileo
Shelagh Delaney	*A Taste of Honey*
	The Lion in Love
Max Frisch	*The Fire Raisers*
	Andorra

Methuen Playscripts

Methuen's Theatre Classics

.ING ALFRED'S COLLEGE
LIBRARY